CW00729720

THE WORLD'S MOST
HORRIFIC
DISASTERS

THE WORLD'S MOST
HORRIFIC
DISASTERS

BY

Nigel Blundell

SUNBURST BOOKS

PHOTOGRAPHY CREDITS

Kubis Heinrich: 25.

Associated Press: 49 (top), 71 (top), 91, 93, 127 (top), 155, 163, 171, 185.

Express Newspapers Plc: 49 (bottom), 71 (bottom), 133, 145 (top), 151 (bottom).

Press Association: 63 (top), 181.

Keystone Press: 63 (bottom).

UPI: 77.

Reuters: 141, 145 (bottom).

Wilkinson: 150, 151 (top).

Copyright unknown: 127 (bottom), 167.

Copyright text © Nigel Blundell 1995
Copyright design © Sunburst Books 1995

This edition published 1995 by Sunburst Books, Deacon House, 65 Old Church Street, London SW3 5BS

The right of Nigel Blundell to be identified as the author of this work has been asserted in accordance with the Copyright, Designs and Patents Act 1988.

All rights reserved. No part of this publication may be reproduced, stored in a retrieval system, or transmitted in any form or by any means, electronic, mechanical, photocopying, recording or otherwise, without the prior written permission of the publishers.

ISBN 1 85778 067 1

Printed and bound in the United Kingdom

Contents

Introduction

Whether man-made, or the product of nature's awesome forces, there is a disturbing fascination about disasters. Perhaps it is because they remind us of our own mortality; that one day we too could be in the wrong place at the wrong time.

Who can say, after news of a plane disaster, that they haven't imagined themselves in the stricken plane, shuddered at the thought of the chaos and panic and the gnawing fear that death must be close?

In this book the appalling carnage of the Tenerife air disaster bears powerful witness to the horror of man-made tragedy. The explosion aboard the Challenger space shuttle is described in detail: how engineers pleaded for the launch to be postponed and how seven astronauts met their death.

Who can forget the horrors of Aberfan in which so many schoolchildren were buried alive?

And there are the natural catastrophes – the San Francisco earthquakes, the Florence floods, and Australian bushfires.

This book is indeed a catalogue of disaster. Yet its pages also recall many examples of the courage and spirit with which men and women face disaster and win through.

Great Fire of London

John Farynor, baker by royal appointment, had just ended another long day sweating amid the heat of his ovens. He felt exhausted as he climbed the stairs above his shop in London's Pudding Lane, too exhausted to care whether everything had been properly cleared up below. As he snuffed out his candle, his only thought was to get a good night's sleep.

It was a forlorn hope. Even as the flame in Farynor's room died, another in the bakery oven flickered into life. His failure to damp the bread ovens was about to start the most famous inferno in history – the Great Fire of London.

At 2 am on Sunday 2 September 1666, the baker scrambled out of his house to see sparks streaming above him. Some of these landed on a pile of dry hay lying outside the nearby Star pub and soon both buildings were well alight. By 3 am the narrow, cramped streets of old London were buzzing with gawping locals.

There was no sign of panic. Fires were not unusual in the Pudding Lane area, where timbers were preserved in highly flammable pitch and the walls were of tinder-dry lathe and plaster. The potential fire hazard had not escaped the attention of King Charles II however. The previous year he had written to city worthies asking them to impose tougher fire regulations. The request had been largely ignored.

Certainly the Lord Mayor was far from impressed when he was woken in the early hours and informed of the Pudding Lane blaze. Aides apologised but insisted that because of the fire's proximity to the main London Bridge road, his Lordship ought to be made aware of the situation. On arrival his Lordship was scathing. 'Pish,' he said, 'a woman might piss it out.'

He was spectacularly wrong. By late afternoon the blaze was licking around the banks of the Thames and was fast spreading westward on a dry easterly wind. Three days later it had already engulfed 87 churches and 13,000 homes as well as the city's financial hub, the Royal Exchange. St. Paul's Cathedral was turned into a gigantic oven, its magnificent stonework exploding and popping under the intense heat. The lead roof melted, dripping into rivers on the streets below.

Amazingly, only eight people died in the fire. Londoners could see for themselves the danger it spelt and they had enough warning to toss their most prized possessions into carts or sacks and head for the countryside.

The diarist Samuel Pepys was among them. Later he wrote: 'With one's face in the wind, you were almost burned with a shower of fire drops (from this) most horrid, malicious, bloody flame.' He added that spiralling above the firestorm was 'a smoke so great as darkened the sun at midday. If at any time the sun peeped forth it looked red like blood'.

Thanks to the personal intervention of the king, who organised gangs to knock down fire-breaks, the worst of the blaze was over by Wednesday evening. Despite this, the city continued to smoulder for a month. Some cellars were still burning six months later.

Farynor may have been directly to blame for the disaster but he also deserves some credit. The fire demolished at a stroke the appalling slums that prevailed in central London and destroyed many of the rats which had spread the Great Plague the previous year.

The Titanic

The 'unsinkable' *Titanic* steamed across the Atlantic on her maiden voyage in 1912, her bands playing, her ballrooms filled, her barmen preparing the most elaborate cocktails and her chefs the most succulent dishes. The cream of British and American society were aboard for the voyage of a lifetime.

After the pomp and partying of its departure from Southampton, it stopped briefly at Cherbourg and at Cobh, Cork. Then, on the evening of Thursday 11 April, it headed out into the Atlantic.

The *Titanic*'s 46,329 tonnes sliced easily through the calm waters, the huge turbines driving her forward at a 'full speed ahead' of 21.5 knots. The 2206 passengers and crew were secure in the knowledge that the liner boasted not only luxury beyond belief but also state-of-the-art safety measures. The massive liner had a double-bottom in the unlikely event that it might hit an iceberg. It had fifteen transverse bulkheads running the length of the vessel to isolate incoming water in the unlikely event of it springing a leak. In the light of these safety measures, the owners of the *Titanic*, the White Star line, had deemed it unnecessary to carry sufficient lifeboats to cater for all the passengers and crew. After all, who would ever need them in such an unsinkable ship.

During the morning of 14 April the temperature dropped suddenly and the captain, Edward Smith, was warned by his radio operators that there were icebergs in the region. The *Titanic* did not drop speed; there was the promised prestige of an award-winning, swift passage to America with a welcoming committee waiting in New York.

Shortly before midnight, the lookout shouted: 'Iceberg right ahead.'

'Hard a-port,' ordered the bridge. But it was too late. As the bow of the ship began to swing to port, an immense iceberg scraped along her starboard side below the water line. There was barely a jolt to disturb the partying passengers or awake those who had retired to their cabins. The officers on the bridge watched the dim shape of the iceberg slip away to their stern.

Captain Smith, who had been relaxing elsewhere in the ship, raced to his post. He arrived on the bridge as the first officer was ordering: 'Stop engines.' Captain Smith sent below for damage reports and could hardly believe his ears when he was told that a huge rent had been torn down the side of the liner. Water was pouring in at an alarming rate – and the watertight bulkheads, in which so much faith had been placed, were now breached. The greatest liner the world had ever seen was sinking.

Throughout the drama being enacted high on the bridge, the liner's passengers were blissfully unaware of the peril they were facing. So gentle had been the collision that few of them had even commented on it. Some of the more energetic wandered onto the open decks and picked up bits of ice to freshen their glasses of whisky. One group even began a snowball fight with debris that had been blown off the passing iceberg.

Captain Smith was a highly experienced skipper. He reacted calmly to the knowledge that a death knell had been sounded for the liner with which he had been entrusted. He ordered the radio room to put out distress calls. Later he had the lifeboats uncovered and made ready while the passengers were raised from their peaceful slumbers by apologetic knocks on their cabin doors. Only then did he authorise distress rockets to be launched.

As the bleary-eyed passengers arrived on deck, the lifeboats were swung out and the order passed down the line: 'Women and children first.' Only now was there the first hint of panic among the passengers. Even the crew were in confusion, never having performed a full boat drill during sea trials. They failed to find many of the collapsible liferafts, which had been stowed in inaccessible places; even when the crew uncovered the rafts, they did not know how to assemble them. There was total confusion: milling around, shouting and screaming – all the sounds associated with panic among men and women who feared they were about to die.

Meanwhile, the radio operators had alerted two other liners to the *Titanic*'s plight. One was the *Frankfort* and the other the *Carpathia*. The captain of the latter was so amazed at the news that the *Titanic* was in trouble that he twice asked his radio operators whether they had got the message right. When assured that they had, and believing that his vessel was closest to the *Titanic*, he ordered his engine room: 'Give it everything we have.'

The *Carpathia*, however, was all of 60 miles away. Much closer was another liner, the *California*, which was only nineteen miles from the *Titanic*. Aboard the *California*, the *Titanic*'s distress flares had been seen by crewmen, who had reported them to the bridge – but who had then been told that they must either be celebratory rockets or a false alarm. The *California* remained stationary as the *Titanic* slowly sank. Captain Stanley Lord insisted until his dying day that his ship had not seen the *Titanic*, and that he could not have arrived in time to save lives. He admitted in evidence that rockets had been seen but that they were taken to be company signals.

It was now around 2 am and the bows of the *Titanic* were beginning to dip lower in the icy black sea. The lifeboats which had been filled, but not lowered in the hope of rescue, were now sent down to the calm waters below. Because many wives had refused to leave their husbands, many of the lifeboats were only half full.

One of the ship's bands continued to play *Nearer My God To Thee* and the reassuring sound wafted across the black sea as women in the lifeboats watched the men waving from the decks high above them.

Captain Smith, having now realised that no other vessel was coming to his aid, ordered: 'Abandon ship!'

The *Titanic* was at an almost 90-degree angle in the ocean, her lights still twinkling and reflecting on the lifeboats drifting away from the final horror shortly to come. As if wanting to escape their inevitable fate for just a few seconds longer, some of those who had not got into the lifeboats scrambled up the decks like mountaineers to reach the doomed ship's stern, pointing upwards like a skyscraper.

At 2.20 am she went down. There was a rumble of machinery crashing from stern to bow, then a hissing and bubbling as the boilers exploded. As the *Titanic* descended through 13,000 feet of water, a giant vortex was created which sucked debris and bodies into the depths. Those in the water who were not dragged down by the whirlpool did not drown; they died of cold within two minutes of hitting the water. On the surface, newly-widowed women wept in the bitterly cold night air.

At 4 am the *Carpathia* arrived and took aboard all those in the lifeboats. The exact death toll is not known. According to the official British figures, there were 711 survivors from a total number of 2,201 crew and passengers.

The Royal Scots
Train Crash

The dawn of 22 May 1915 instilled a sense of sadness, fear and excitement in the 500 brave soldiers of the 1/7th battalion, the Royal Scots.

That morning they clambered onto a troop train at Larbet Station in Scotland for the long journey south. Ahead lay the trenches and battlefields of Western Europe and the likely prospect of dying for their country. For some of the fresh-faced youths it was their first venture outside Scotland.

Tragically, for many, it would also be their last. They would die sooner than their blackest nightmares predicted – merely a few minutes ride from the Scottish border. And all because two signal men were intent on bending the rules for swapping shifts.

The disaster which befell the special troop train ranks among the worst rail crashes in British history. Fate undoubtedly played a part, yet had procedures been followed properly the railmen concerned would probably have handled the trains safely and competently. As in so many transport disasters, however, an element of complacency had crept in.

The troop train was due to travel down a 1:200 line gradient, past a remote signals box at Quintinshill and on to Carlisle. From there its destination in England was top secret. Spies, the soldiers had been told, were everywhere.

Northbound express traffic that morning was running late. Both the 11.45 pm London Euston to Edinburgh sleeper and the midnight Euston to Glasgow sleeper had fallen half-an-hour behind schedule. They were not expected to pull out of Carlisle station until 5.50 am and 6.05 am respectively, even though the drivers would be pushing their locomotives hard to make up time. The London and North-Western Railway took great pride in its punctuality.

So did the Caledonian Railway. It ran an all-stations, 'slow local' train between Carlisle and Beattock using the same northbound line as the express trains pounding up from London. Affectionately known as the *Parley* among the locals, this train was due to leave Carlisle at 6.10 am. It then had to reach Beattock by 7.49 am to make a connection.

If the sleepers were on time, the arrangement went without a hitch. But if they were late – as they so often were – the *Parley* had to be held back to ensure the line north was clear. In recent months Caledonian officials had found a way around this conundrum by starting the *Parley* off ahead of the London trains and then shunting it into sidings at Quintinshill to let them pass. This manoeuvre had been taking place on average once a week for the past six months.

There were certainly no complaints from the two signal men, Tinsley and Meakin, who manned the Quintinshill box. Usually they had to walk the mile and a half to work from Gretna, where they both lived. But on mornings when the *Parley* was going to be sidelined, they could get a ride on the footplate and jump off when the train stopped at their box. All they had to do was check with the Gretna signal man beforehand to find out whether the London trains were on time.

There was one snag with this piece of rule-bending. Tinsley and Meakin were supposed to swap shifts at 6 am, although the *Parley* never got to Quintinshill before 6.13 am. It meant that whoever had worked the night shift had to stop entering information in the train register at 6 am and log any entries for the next fifteen minutes on a separate sheet of paper. The day shift man would then copy the entries into the register as soon as he arrived.

The aim was to deceive any nosy official who might check the register. From 6 am every day the handwriting would always alter – proof that the change-over had taken place according to the rules and regulations.

At 6.10 am on 22 May, Tinsley boarded the *Parley* train at Gretna, knowing that it would divert into the Quintinshill northbound siding. However, when they reached the relevant set of points it became clear this was impossible. A goods train had been shunted onto the siding to await collection and there was no room to fit in the *Parley* as well. Tinsley decided he would have to direct the *Parley* off the northbound line and onto the main southbound track until the two London-Scotland services had passed.

This was not a particularly unusual or dangerous operation. It had been accomplished four times in the last six months with no problems. The most important thing was for the signal box immediately north of Quintinshill, at Kirkpatrick, to be kept informed.

At 6.38 the Edinburgh-bound express passed safely. But soon afterwards the situation took a more complex twist when a southbound goods train pulling empty coal wagons turned up. The driver was ordered into the southbound siding to await instructions.

To summarise, the sight from the Quintinshill box was now as follows:

Northbound siding: Goods train. Northbound main line: Clear. Southbound main line: *Parley* train. Southbound siding: Empty coal train.

Tinsley was by now in the signal box copying

Meakin's notes into the train register. Meakin had stayed on in the signal box for a few moments to read his colleague's newspaper and talk about the progress of the war. Neither man was really concentrating on the trains.

Sometime in the next few minutes one of the pair (both later denied it) sent a message to the Kirkpatrick box advising that the coal train had been shunted off the southbound main line. Crucially, that message made no mention of the fact that the *Parley* train had been shunted on to it earlier. Tinsley and Meakin had also failed to pull the levers controlling the southbound track into their protective collars. This would have provided a visible reminder that the line could not be used. The die for disaster was now cast.

At 6.42 am Kirkpatrick offered Quintinshill control of the troop train. Without even glancing out of the window, and barely pausing in his chatter with Meakin, Tinsley accepted it and pulled all the southbound levers to show the line ahead was free. Hardly had he returned to his copying when Gretna offered him the late-running Glasgow express. Again Tinsley agreed to take it under his control and pulled all northbound signals to the 'clear' position.

Meanwhile the *Parley* sat on the southbound line, brakes locked, a doomed train awaiting terrible destruction.

A minute later the troop train rounded the downhill curve into Quintinshill and cannoned into the *Parley* at 70 mph. The impact had a devastating affect on the soldiers' carriages, squashing them from a total length of 237 yards down to 67 yards. Both trains lay buried beneath their coaches, many of which had spilled onto the northbound express track. And then, topping 60 mph, the Glasgow-bound express smashed into this scene of carnage.

The exact death toll will probably never be known. Wartime restrictions on information meant the full horror of the pile-up was suppressed and official figures claimed an unlikely 215 soldiers dead and 191 injured. In fact, of the 500 who began that dreadful journey from Larbet only 52 survivors were accounted for. Civilian casualties at least were miraculously light – just ten dead and 51 injured.

Meakin and Tinsley each served lengthy jail terms after being convicted of manslaughter. There were many in the country who would cheerfully have hanged them.

The Hindenburg and R101

The airship *Hindenburg* was to the skies what the *Titanic* was to the seas. She excelled in grandeur and style, and boasted every safety feature of her age. And like the great ship which was doomed to die on an Atlantic crossing, the *Hindenburg* met her end after crossing the ocean, transformed in seconds from a graceful cigar-shaped floating palace into a burning hell.

Her dreadful demise, coming only seven years after the crash of the British airship the *R101*, finally rang the death knell for this gracious and glamorous form of air travel.

The story of the *Hindenburg* begins in 1935 when the airship was completed, although its first test flight was not until 1936. It was the largest, most luxurious dirigible ever made and was a proud showpiece of Hitler's Germany – a symbol of Aryan superiority and a statement to the world that the age of the airship was here to stay.

The vessel had a proud record to live up to: there had never been a fatality in German civil airship travel, and the safety standards were of the highest. Because of the inflammable hydrogen inside the *Hindenburg*'s sixteen huge gas cells, every crew member wore anti-static asbestos-

Lakehurst, New Jersey, 1937. After successfully crossing the Atlantic, the once-graceful airship Hindenburg explodes in a ball of flames infront of relatives of the passengers onboard.

impregnated overalls and shoes soled with hemp. All crew members had to hand in matches and lighters before embarking, as did all passengers. If guests wished to smoke they were seated in a special pressurised lounge. A steward performed the function of lighting their cigars or cigarettes in another room, sealed off by a double-door and out of bounds to passengers.

There were sophisticated insulation devices and warning systems to detect any leakages of gas. The *Hindenburg* could have flown on harmless helium, but the only nation producing sufficient quantities of it in those days was the USA – and they withheld it from Hitler's Germany as the war clouds gathered in case it was used for his military machine. Apart from that one drawback, every eventuality had been catered for – or so the designers thought.

The quality of the safety precautions was equalled only by the splendour of the state rooms, the dining room, the lounge and bar. There was even a lightweight piano, specially made from aluminium, to entertain the 35 passengers. And, of course, there were superb meals and wines, served by chefs and waiters trained in Europe's finest establishments.

The transatlantic runs of the *Hindenburg* (the airship was named after one of Germany's greatest generals) went without a hitch in 1936.

Throughout that year, she glided effortlessly from her base at Frankfurt across the Atlantic and back under the expert command of Max Pruss, a seasoned Zeppelin commander.

But on 6 May 1937, as the *Hindenburg* approached Lakehurst naval station, New Jersey, on the final leg of its journey, the unthinkable happened. Within seconds of the guide-ropes being lowered for landing, flames erupted from the body of the great airship. From stem to stern, the *Hindenburg*, filled with 198,000 cubic metres of highly inflammable hydrogen gas, was gutted by fire.

The best testimony to the tragic event was provided by a radio reporter who was broadcasting the landing live to the American nation. His emotional speech has since gone down in the annals of history.

Herbert Morrison was watching the night sky with studious indifference. The airship was running ten hours late because of bad weather and Commander Pruss delayed the landing still more because of unfavourable rain, wind and cloud conditions, coupled with poor visibility. Finally he moved in. Morrison reported:

'The ropes have been dropped and they have been taken hold of by a number of men in the field. The back motors of the ship are holding it just enough to keep it . . . It's burst into flame!

This is terrible . . . the flames are 500 feet into the sky . . . it is in smoke and flames now, those passengers . . . I'm going to have to step inside where I can't see it. I . . . I . . . folks, I'm going to have to stop for a while. This is the worst thing I've ever witnessed. It is one of the worst catastrophes in the world.'

This was the choked voice of Morrison as he described the demise of the *Hindenburg*. Other eye-witnesses recall the belly of the ship glowing red before sheet-flame broke from the tail. The night air was filled with the hissing of fire as it swept through the gas-filled ship. Explosions could be heard up to fifteen miles away as, one by one, the giant gas-bags exploded.

It was a nightmarish scene as passengers and crewmen jumped from windows and doors while the ship thrashed in her final agony.

Commander Pruss stayed at his controls in the command gondola until the ship hit the ground. He survived but his first captain, Ernst Lehmann, was mortally injured. He was found crouching in the glowing rubble, mumbling over and over: 'I don't understand, I don't understand.'

The enormous airship had been destroyed in just 32 seconds from a cause still unknown. Miraculously, 62 of the 97 passengers and crew lived. The dead numbered twenty crewmen and fifteen passengers.

What also died forever that day was the dream of intercontinental air travel by the beautiful and silent leviathans of the sky.

The *Hindenburg* was not the first airship to fall from the sky. The *R101*, the largest flying machine in the world, 200 yards long and filled with 5,000,000 cubic feet of hydrogen, lumbered into the sky at Cardington, Bedfordshire, on the wet and miserable evening of 4 October 1930. Aboard were 48 crew and 6 passengers, among the latter being Lord Thomson, Her Majesty's noble Air Minister – and stubborn fool.

The soon-to-be-infamous Lord Thomson was the man responsible for the *R101*. So fanatical was he about his aerial dream that he adopted the name of the nationalised aircraft factory as part of his title. It was therefore Lord Thomson of Cardington who oversaw the building of the airship at Cardington, near Bedford. And so arrogant was he that he stolidly pushed his pet project to its perilous conclusion, despite warnings galore about the desperately unsafe state of the *R101*.

The gas valves were so sensitive that they leaked perpetually. The propellers broke when put into reverse, and a heavy backward-facing engine had to be fitted in order that the airship could manoeuvre when docking. The hydrogen bags which would keep it aloft rolled around inside the craft. The airship was unbalanced – it bucked up and down dangerously as soon as it was tethered at its mooring mast.

The *R101*'s outer casing split time and time again. The craft emerged from its hangar one day with a rip 50 yards long in its side. It was repaired but exactly the same thing occurred the following day. The airship ended up being covered with patches, and the fins, though beautifully streamlined, tended to stall.

In an attempt to solve the problems, Air Ministry technicians cut the airship in two, inserted an extra gas tank in the middle, put the craft together again and once again hauled it to its mooring tower. Minutes later, however, the whole skin of the airship began rippling in the wind, and a 90-foot gash opened along its side. The next step was to begin disposing of every piece of non-essential equipment – so out went all the luxurious touches which Lord Thomson had been so proud of.

On 28 June 1930 the mighty dirigible was flown to Hendon to take part in an air display – and immediately appeared to embark on a sequence of aerial stunts. It twisted and turned, then suddenly dipped its nose and dived spectacularly before pulling up sharply. Only a few moments later the aircraft, already much too low for comfort, repeated the manoeuvre and pulled out of its dive just 500 feet above the ground. The 100,000-strong crowd applauded, unaware that the dramatic show had, of course, been entirely unplanned. In fact, the craft's sweating coxswain had been struggling at the controls to avert disaster. Neither were the public ever told that when the *R101* was examined afterwards, more than 60 holes were found in the hydrogen bags. The highly inflammable gas was pouring out everywhere.

All these problems were swiftly brushed under the table by Lord Thomson. Despite dissent among many of the designers, fears by Air Ministry inspectors and the alarm of the Cardington team itself, the great man would not be swayed. Lord Thomson had other reasons for pressing ahead his personal flight to India. He wanted to make a magnificent impression when the airship arrived at Karachi. His ambition was to become Viceroy of India and he hoped that the spectacle would help him achieve that aim. And he had to fly straightaway because he did not want to miss the Imperial Conference to be held in London in mid-October.

Lord Thomson announced: 'The *R101* is as safe as a house, at least to the millionth chance.' He issued an official directive: 'I must insist on the programme for the Indian flight being adhered to, as I have made my plans accordingly.'

And so, re-covered, lightened and even lengthened, the *R101* embarked upon its trial flight on 1 October 1930. The craft's oil-cooler having broken down, there was no opportunity for any speed trials, poor-weather tests had not even been attempted, and the airship had not flown at full power. Neither had the *R101* been issued with an Airworthiness Certificate. That was simply solved: the Air Ministry wrote one out for themselves.

The flight date to India was set for 4 October. The very day before, Lord Thomson piously warned a conference at his Air Ministry: 'You must not allow my natural impatience or anxiety to influence you in any way.'

Author Nevil Shute, himself an engineer then involved in a rival airship project, wrote later: 'To us, watching helplessly on the sidelines, the decision to fly the *R101* to India that autumn of 1930 appeared to be sheer midsummer madness.' He said of Thomson: 'He was the man primarily responsible for the organisation which produced the disaster. Under his control, practically every principle of safety in the air was abandoned.'

Lord Thomson proudly boarded the *R101*, with by his valet, at 6.30 pm on 4 October. Agonisingly slowly, the craft left its mooring mast and headed for London on its route across the English Channel and over France.

As the rain lashed down on the airship, the weight of tonnes of water slowed it and made it even more unstable. It rolled and pitched and was flying dangerously low. As the craft crossed the Channel, the watch noticed the surging seas perilously close below. An officer grabbed the controls and brought the *R101* back to 1000 feet.

The *R101* crossed the French coast and observers estimated her height at only 300 feet. At 2 am with the wind increasing, the *R101* was over Beauvais, having travelled only 200 miles in more than seven hours. It was then that the nose of the *R101* suddenly dipped.

Below in Beauvais, several citizens were leaning out of their windows watching the strange airship sail by. It passed over the centre of the town, about 200 yards above the ground. It was pitching and rolling. The coxswain wrestled with the controls. The elevators did not respond. The frail fabric at the nose of the ship had split. The wind was gusting in and the hydrogen was pouring out.

Peering at the looming earth through the window of the control room, the first officer realised the airship was doomed. Another brave officer raced through the hull in a bid to alert everyone that the ship was about to crash. The slumbering passengers and crew heard him screaming over and over: 'We're down lads!'

Another valiant crewman remained at his post to pull at the wheel governing the elevators in a bid to make the craft climb. He died at his post – but thanks to his efforts, the *R101* touched down lightly. One or two bodies fell from one of the gondolas onto the soggy ground.

There was a gush of escaping gas, then a blinding flash lit the sky. Two further explosions quickly followed and a white-hot inferno engulfed the *R101*. Of the 54 people who had boarded the airship in England, only 6 survived. Lord Thomson of Cardington was among the 48 who perished.

Sheltering in nearby woods, a poacher, 56-year-old Alfred Roubaille, witnessed the entire catastrophe. 'I heard people in the wreckage crying for help,' he recalled. 'I was a hundred yards away and the heat was awful. I ran as hard as I could away from that place.'

The Black Market Express

It was a freezing night as Train No. 8017 began its regular Thursday night run between the Italian cities of Naples and Lucania. Every carriage of the train was packed, as usual. This was wartime and many of the 520 passengers aboard were planning to buy up as much meat, cooking oil, tobacco and sweets as they could possibly lay their hands on in Lucania. The 8017 was not nicknamed the 'Black Market Express' for nothing.

The Allied Military Government which ran Italy knew exactly what was going on. Under-the-counter deals were strictly prohibited, nonetheless officials generally turned a blind eye to the black marketeers. If the marketeers didn't ply their trade, the million-plus inhabitants of Naples would undoubtedly be pushed close to starvation. The last thing the government needed was unrest on the streets.

This particular night – 2 March 1944 – the 8017 was heavier than usual. The four coaches, caboose and 42 empty box cars were being pulled by two steam engines, considered powerful enough for a maximum load of 500 tonnes. At Naples, however, a big party of medical students embarked, together with the equipment they had used on a field exercise near Bari. That pushed the total weight of the *Black Market Express* to 511 tonnes.

Chief engineer Gigliani, in the lead engine, was not unduly concerned by the overloading. But he knew it would be a busy night. The track ahead led through the Apennine Mountains where some of the gradients would be extremely steep and the rails coated with ice. Gigliani knew he would have to hit top speed well before these sections to have any chance of climbing them. The stokers would have to keep fires well fuelled.

At Belvano-Ricigliano station Gigliani ordered his fireman, Rosario Barbato, to shovel a huge pile of fuel into the furnaces. 'We'll need it for these up gradients later,' he explained.

During those few minutes at Belvano one passenger, olive-oil salesman Domenico Miele, took the opportunity to stretch his legs. A few lungfuls of the icy night air made him wide awake and he rummaged through his luggage for a scarf to keep him warm.

His decision to step off the express saved his life. When he took his seat again he noticed that almost all of his fellow passengers were asleep.

Miele's next recollection was suffering a fit of coughing soon after the train entered a tunnel. He clambered off, using his scarf as a filter, and tottered down the line with the intention of finding a seat in a less smoky carriage. He made it to the vestibule of the last carriage before collapsing unconscious.

Since leaving Belvano the engines had successfully negotiated two tunnels on moderate gradients. They pulled powerfully along a 25-yard viaduct and then entered the winding, two-mile long Galleria delle Armi tunnel beneath a mountain forest. Here though, the engines quickly began to slow. Just before the final car, the caboose, disappeared into the mountain, the train ground to a halt.

In the caboose, brakeman Michele Palo thought the drivers had a signal against them. He had heard no warning and therefore assumed that everything was in order. However, when there was no progress after several minutes he lost patience, pulled on his gloves and headed into the tunnel to find out what was going on. The sight that greeted him would haunt him for the rest of his days.

Gibbering, Palo scrambled back down the track and began half-running, half-crawling towards Belvano station. He hoped the journey might take an hour, still time to get help for his fellow passengers. But he was hopelessly optimistic. The icy track and the pitch-black tunnels meant it would take him twice that time to raise the alarm.

Meanwhile, back at Belvano, the night duty assistant station master Giuseppe Salonia was settled in his office with a newspaper. Having seen off the 8017 he had well over an hour before the 8025 steamed in.

It was not until 2.30 am that he realised the next up-line station, Bella-Muro, had failed to inform him of the 8017's arrival. Impatiently, Salonia called them to remonstrate. The answer he got left the words frozen on his lips. Number 8017 had not arrived at Bella-Muro. It was nearly two hours late. Salonia told his colleagues he would hold the 8025 at Belvano and check the line himself with one of its locomotives.

Hardly had he clambered aboard this engine when he saw Michele Palo emerging from the nearest tunnel swinging a red lantern. As Salonia reached him he collapsed, begging for help to be directed up the track. Salonia asked him again what was wrong. 'Soni tutti morti!' moaned Palo ('They're all dead').

But Salonia had no evidence of an accident. He reasoned that any crash or collision would surely have been heard across the quiet, snow-covered countryside. Perhaps the weeping brakeman had just taken leave of his senses. Mystified, Salonia picked the man up in his arms and gently carried him back to Belvano to try to uncover the truth.

Once in the warmth of the station, Palo calmed down and gave a more lucid account of his ordeal. All the same, his words stretched credulity to the limit. Every passenger dead? How was it possible? Although it was 4 am Salonia decided he had to rouse police and the local military officials. Then he set off up the track in the borrowed engine from the 8025.

When he opened the door of one coach it was like a scene from a horror movie. Some passengers were seated, some sprawled on the floor, some leaning against each other. All of them looked asleep, their faces calm and relaxed. Salonia could tell instantly they were dead. In the engine cabs it was the same story. One of the engineers still held his hand on the throttle, his head resting on the window.

Tears streaming down his face, Salonia backed his locomotive onto Palo's caboose. Then he towed the ghost train with its coachloads of corpses back to Belvano where stunned police officers began carrying the bodies to a temporary mortuary. The death toll was 516 passengers and four railwaymen.

Only five people survived. One of them was Domenico Miele, taken for dead by police, but later recovered sufficiently to give his account of what happened. Three other survivors sloped quietly away, perhaps concerned that their black market activities would come under scrutiny. The fifth appeared so badly brain damaged that he had no idea who or where he was, or even that his wife and eight-year-old son were among the many dead.

So what had happened to the doomed night train. From Miele, Palo and Salonia's accounts, state police concluded that No. 8017 could not have penetrated very far into the Galleria delle Armi tunnel before its wheels began to slide on the icy gradient. The engineer Gigliani could have reversed out and onto the viaduct. Instead he ordered his crew to restoke the fires in an attempt to marshall enough power to climb the incline. He and stoker Barbato piled the soft coal into the leading loco, while behind them throttler Senatore and foreman Ronga sweated and strained to do their bit. It was all to no avail. The wheels rotated faster but they could not grip.

Not one of the four men toiling in the flickering light of the furnaces could have realised they were signing their own death warrants. In the confined space of the tunnel, deadly carbon monoxide fumes enveloped first the two locomotives and then slowly seeped back to gas the passengers. No one ever suspected danger. Most were asleep and the few who did stir registered only that the express had stopped in pitch blackness.

The tragic story was never properly told until after the war ended. Censorship restricted information to a short official report about the sad 'mishap' which befell Train 8017. Neither was there any compensation or redress for the families of the dead. The military government deemed it was a 'wartime accident'. As such, it washed its hands of all responsibility.

The Lakonia

The cruise ship *Lakonia* was like an old lady, made up and thrust back into the limelight as a glamour girl.

She had been built in 1930 in Amsterdam and saw service during the war as a troop ship operating across the Atlantic and around the Mediterranean. Later she regularly tramped the slow, arduous route to Australia and New Zealand, ferrying immigrants, but when the rush to the southern hemisphere began to fizzle out she was sold to new owners.

In 1963 she was bought by The Greek Line. The company's plan was to give her a facelift and launch her in the lucrative winter cruise market between Southampton and the Canary Islands. On 19 December, 650 mostly elderly passengers began to board the ship. Many were eagerly looking forward to their first Christmas at sea and were far too excited to notice the ship's shortcomings. Yet the more experienced passengers immediately had their doubts as they strolled the decks.

Soon the poor purser was fielding complaint after complaint – and the ship had not even left the dockside. He prayed that none of the passengers would notice the repair men coming out of the engine room at 5 pm. To put it mildly, the *Lakonia* was not quite as advertised in her glitzy brochures.

One of those disillusioned passengers was Joseph Wright, a retired company director and qualified engineer. He and his wife had arrived in their cabin to find it freezing and devoid of hot water. Unimpressed by what he'd seen, he decided to make a closer inspection of the 20,238 tonne cruise liner.

What Mr Wright found left him incredulous. Most of the lifeboats were old and worn with planks so badly sprung 'you could have pushed a penny between them'. The lack of lubrication and spread of rust suggested many of the boats hadn't been tested or swung out in years. 'God help us if we have to go down in these,' he told his wife.

Another passenger, Harry Craige of Putney, south London, was so troubled by the state of the lifeboats that he resolved to disembark the *Lakonia* as soon as possible. 'I don't think we'll come back on this ship,' he said to his wife. 'I don't like it at all. I'm going to the wireless office to send a cable to Cook's (his travel agent). We'll cancel our return trip and come home by plane from Las Palmas.'

The Greek captain, Mathios Zarbis, was aware of the rumblings of discontent on board. He had been the obvious choice as master, not just for his seamanship but also for his warm and engaging personality. He began a charm offensive, laughing and chatting with the ladies and singling out couples who might conceivably take their complaints further. By the time they reached the waters around Madeira on the 22 December he was using the evening's fancy dress ball to win over any remaining doubters. Both the Craiges and the Wrights found themselves sitting at his table.

Zarbis had just finished whirling Mrs Wright around the dance floor when a crew member hurtled into the ballroom. 'Captain,' he cried, 'fire reported in the hairdresser's salon.' Smiling his excuses – and inwardly cursing – Zarbis left to find out what had happened.

It was already too late to save his ship. With her upper decks and cabins built almost entirely of wood, a multi-national crew untrained to handle an emergency and a complete breakdown of the public address system, passengers resorted to taking – or ignoring – advice from each other. When one man rushed into the ship's cinema to raise the alarm he was treated as a drunk. Most of the audience carried on watching Bob Hope in *Call Me Bwana*.

Yet amid the chaos, some of the crew excelled themselves. A young Greek Cypriot steward called Andre Vasilades volunteered to go over the side suspended on a thin cord to rescue ten-year-old Nicolas Fishenden who was trapped in his cabin. As the steward hung outside the porthole the little boy cried: 'I don't know what to do.'

'You don't have to do anything,' Vasilades told him gently, 'just give me your right hand.'

Nicolas was pulled to safety, only to die minutes later when he and his mother were tipped from a lifeboat as it was being lowered. The boat fell on them as they floundered in the waves.

Now the blazing ship was a writhing mass of chaos and confusion. Yet amazingly there was little sign of panic. Many of those aboard were Britons with vivid memories of World War II battles and the Blitz. Some sat on the upper decks calmly playing cards. Others enjoyed free drinks from the bar and sampled slices of prime salmon. As they sat incongruously in their 'tramps ball' fancy dress outfits, few could comprehend how rapidly they had become imperilled.

By the early hours, however, it was impossible to ignore the danger any longer. Passengers unable to find an operational lifeboat faced a choice between throwing themselves into the sea or roasting alive. When the cinema exploded, even the optimistic Captain Zarbis lost his last vestiges of hope.

The first of the survivors were winched aboard the Argentinian liner, *Salta*, at about 4.30 am on

23 December. One by one, other ships such as the British *Montcalm*, the United States freighter *Rio Grande*, the *Charlesville* from Belgium and the Pakistani-registered *Mehdi* answered Captain Zarbis's SOS signal.

At 7.30 am the situation for those remaining on board was desperate. These last passengers were mainly the elderly and infirm – people who could not face the 30 foot drop to the waves below. The cruise director George Herbert, one of the many crew members who stayed with them, later admitted: 'I found it a most harrowing affair. They were old people, obviously in many cases incapable of fending for themselves in the water. I felt I was pushing some of them to their deaths. I am sure I did.'

Eye-witness Reg Fishenden – who had watched in anguish as his wife and son were killed by a falling lifeboat – later recalled:

'They were coming down in their dozens and I saw them passing me. Some of the old ones were falling off, screaming, into the water. There was no scrambling and they were quite orderly until they fell. Their cries were terrifying and I thought the best thing I could do was remain where I was. I did not see myself having any chance in the water at all.'

To his credit, Captain Zarbis was the last to leave. It was 10 am before he was satisfied that everyone who could be saved had been saved. Wearily he plunged overboard and sought refuge in a rubber dinghy.

Amazingly, a Greek court later convicted him of manslaughter and sentenced him to fourteen months in prison. It was an outrageous decision. If blame for the 128 lost lives lay anywhere, it lay at the feet of the ship's owners who had allowed the *Lakonia* to sail as a floating death-trap.

The Vaiont Dam

Every weekend, rain or shine, the angling parties would trek up to the Vaiont Dam to enjoy some of the finest lake fishing anywhere in the Italian Alps.

They came not only for the sport. Surrounded on all sides by the dramatic Mount Toc skyline, the dam exuded a sense of peace and calm. On a clear, windless day you could hear a stone splash hundreds of yards away.

During the autumn of 1963, regular visitors might have heard quite a few stones rattling into the lake from above. They didn't pay much heed. It was quite a common phenomenon after rain because of the lubricating effect on mud and rubble. Meteorologists had just recorded one of the wettest Septembers on record.

On the dam itself however, the mini landslides did register with engineers. They were concerned that if a sizeable chunk of the mountain slipped and crashed into the water the resulting shock wave could sweep away anyone standing on the shore. On 8 October a warning was issued urging all anglers, walkers and picnickers to stay off the dam until the situation stabilised.

The V-shaped Vaiont was one of the wonders of Italian engineering. Towering 873 feet over the

The damage to this Italian house bears witness to the force of the 'sea of mud' which swept down upon it.

Italian rescue services search in vain for survivors among the rubble and mud.

Piave River the dam had been commissioned by Italy's state-run electricity industry and formed part of a network of five making up the north-west-Piave hydro-electric power scheme. When it opened in 1960 it was the third biggest concrete dam in the world and an environmentalist's dream come true.

Hydro-electric power is produced by allowing water under enormous pressure to race out through tunnels containing turbines. These turbines are linked to generators which in turn feed the national grid. The initial building costs are high, but once established, hydro-power is cheap, pollution-free and inexhaustible. It is also flexible. When demand for power is high, more turbines are opened. At night they can be shut down allowing the dam to replenish itself from dozens of feeder-streams.

That at least is the theory and for the most part it works perfectly in hundreds of locations around the world. Yet anyone living in the shadow of the giant dams must occasionally ask themselves: 'What if something goes wrong? What if it bursts?'

The villagers downstream of the Vaiont were no exception. The main settlement of Longarone, and its satellite villages of Fae, Pirago, Codissago and Castellavazzo, were sited right in the path of any flood that developed. The locals consoled themselves with the knowledge that the dam had been constructed under government supervision and that a small army of workers monitored it night and day. If anything went wrong, they reasoned, there would be plenty of warning.

In fact, the night disaster struck, there was less than 30 minutes warning. And even then, it was a warning nobody recognised.

At about 10.45 pm, as the lights went out along the Piave valley, an automatic seismic recorder on the 6000 feet high Mount Toc picked up an earth tremor. It was a strong signal, yet incapable of causing widespread damage on its own. Only when the shock-wave penetrated the sodden soil and rubble did it become a killer.

One scientist later drew the following analogy: 'Imagine you are with your kids making sandcastles on the beach. You pack wet sand into a bucket and turn it upside down at an acute angle over a rock pool. The sand sticks, even though it is well lubricated.

'But if you shake the bucket the shock-wave loosens that stability, the sand crashes down into the pool and you get an almighty splash. That was the effect the earth tremor had on the Vaiont Dam, except on a gigantic scale.'

At around 11.15 pm, the gradual slipping and sliding of rubble that had been going on for 30 minutes suddenly turned into one, simultaneous landslide. Thousands upon thousands of tonnes of earth rumbled into the lake forming an island in the centre. Millions of gallons of water was instantly displaced. It had nowhere to go – except over the top of the dam and into the valley below.

Later some of the locals recalled hearing the sound, like rolling thunder only deeper and somehow more sinister. Many believed the dam had ruptured and they grabbed children and a few precious possessions and tore straight out into the night air. Only those lucky enough to live on high ground survived to tell the tale. The rest were swept away in a lethal brown, foaming tide of soil, sticks and rubble.

At daybreak the full, macabre truth became self-evident. An estimated 80 per cent of the buildings in Longarone were destroyed. Everyone living in Fae and Pirago had been drowned and Codissago and Castellavazzo had each lost half their population. Roads were either buried or swept away and telephone and power lines lay uselessly on the ground. As Italy woke up to one of its worst peace time disasters, rescue workers faced the huge task of planning an effective, coordinated relief operation.

One government minister summed up the scene: 'It is a truly biblical disaster,' he said. 'Like Pompeii before the excavations began.'

Throughout the day, worried relatives and

friends descended to the mountain villages desperately seeking news of their loved ones. The sight that greeted them must have chilled their hearts. Naked bodies were heaped next to dead cattle. Other people were hanging from uprooted trees as though on gibbets. And everywhere cadavers were floating in the water, nudging and bumping the legs of rescue workers as though trying to keep a last, futile grip on life.

Town hall officials at nearby Belluno quickly ordered 500 coffins for use in a mass burial ceremony. But within 72 hours it was clear hundreds more were needed. Bodies were being transported by the lorry load or stretchered out of helicopters. Relief workers were ordered to spray them with disinfectant in a primitive attempt to restrict the spread of disease. In fact, many corpses were committed to mass graves on the assumption that they would never be identified.

Putting names to the dead proved almost impossible. The flood had claimed whole families, often their close relatives too. Occasionally, some traumatised helper would turn over a body to stare into the lifeless features of a friend or neighbour. It was like the plot from the worst kind of cheap and nasty horror movie.

The official death toll was put at 1,189 though scores of victims were never found. Survivors were few and far between, although two children were amazingly plucked alive from a cellar under the rubble that was once their home. To their credit, the rescue teams worked round the clock checking every last building – long after any real hope of finding life had been lost.

Inevitably, there were soon bitter recriminations over who was responsible for the disaster. Some politicians questioned whether the dam should ever have been sited in the position chosen. Newspapers reported that more than three years after construction work had finished, geologists were still researching the suitability of the surrounding mountain. Building contractors had encountered several major landslides yet had simply covered up the cracks and fissures with reinforced concrete. And some of the dam technicians who died that dreadful night had spoken openly to friends and family of the imminent disaster.

A government inquiry was damning in its criticism of the local authorities and the electricity industry. It recommended the dam be closed for good and the Italian Parliament quickly agreed. The villages were rebuilt and manufacturers were offered incentives to resite factories in the stricken valley. Today the only reminder of the night five villages died are the plaques and monuments marking mass graves.

Florence Floods

To lovers of Renaissance art, the Italian city of Florence is nothing less than a mecca. Every year, thousands of visitors make a pilgrimage to the beautiful Tuscan capital. They come to marvel at the art treasures – works by the likes of Michelangelo, Donatello, Masaccio, Giotto, Botticelli, Raphael, Titian and Rubens. They come to see the breathtaking Romanesque buildings, the architecture of the thirteenth century Cathedral Sta Maria del Fiore, the campanile of Giotto or the fourteenth century Ponte Vecchio which bridges the River Arno. Or the visitors come simply to soak up the still-magical atmosphere of the streets that inspired so many geniuses.

Yet for all its appearances, the city has not always been such a tranquil haven. During the thirteenth and fourteenth centuries Florence was regularly sacked by feuding families and over the years it has suffered severe war damage (including the effects of World War II). None of these man-made disasters, however, brought about as much destruction as the fury with which the forces of nature treated Florence in November 1966.

Florence had seen floods before, but the autumn storms that hit much of northern and western Europe that year were unprecedented in living memory. Rivers rising in the Alps, Dolomites and Apennines were swollen overnight into mighty torrents which tossed around trees, rocks, boulders and buildings as though they were children's bath toys.

In some areas the equivalent of six month's rain descended in little more than 24 hours. Fuelled by melting snow, and whipped into a ferocious frothing tide by hurricane-force winds, the effect on anything in the water's path was nothing short of catastrophic.

In the north-eastern region of Friuli-Venezia-Giulia farms, homes, roads and railways were washed away in a terrifying cocktail of destruction. Avalanches and mud-slides heightened the chaos and, through it all, the water flowed at ever-increasing rates. Mud deposits were so extensive that many cars and buses were buried beneath them.

In the lush agricultural land of Maremma more than 80 per cent of cattle were either killed or had to be slaughtered. Fruit and root vegetables lay rotting under several feet of water. And in the district capital Grosetto, four-fifths of the streets were submerged underneath millions of gallons of mud and water.

Predictably, Venice was also badly hit. Here the combination of swollen rivers and angry seas resulted in the worst flooding for 1000 years. The 400-year-old dykes linking the islands on which the beautiful city was founded had been poorly maintained for many decades. Now they were no longer up to the job demanded of them. The island of Pellestrina was first to report that a dyke had been breached and within minutes a tidal wave of water seven feet high was raging through the streets. Life in the city was brought to a complete standstill.

Had the floods been pure freshwater, or even sea water, it would have been bad enough. But they weren't. After a day or two raw sewage was seen floating everywhere along with oil which had leaked from central heating storage tanks. Stock held by thousands of shops turned into an insurance write-off and hotels faced a combined repair bill totalling millions of pounds.

Yet if Venice was bad, Florence was much, much worse. On 4 November the River Arno burst its banks, spewing a lethally fast torrent of water into the heart of the city itself. Film shot at the time shows cars riding along in the waves at speeds of up to 40 mph. Cathedral Square and the magnificent Baptistery ended up submerged beneath fifteen feet of water. And all the while the creeping, filthy tide – again streaked with oil and petrol – sought out some of the greatest treasures of Western civilisation.

Almost every famous building on the tourist trail was swamped. The San Firenzi Palace, the Casa di Dante, the Santa Maria Novella and the internationally renowned Uffizi art gallery were among the worst affected. At the Uffizi some 600 masterpieces lay under water for hours. Though they could be restored, 130,000 negatives of Florentine art – including hundreds that were irreplaceable – were beyond help.

As the waters subsided, leaving a legacy of putrid yellow mud, the enormity of the disaster began to dawn on art experts from around the world. Ruined material included Tuscany's civil records covering more than 400 years to 1860, the Archaeological Museum's Etruscan collection, original sheets of music penned by Scarlatti and one of the earliest known examples of Western art, Cimabue's *Crucifixion*, dating from the thirteenth century.

The libraries were just as badly hit. An estimated 6,000,000 old books, including some believed to be unique, became saturated where they lay in vaults beneath the Biblioteca Nazionale. Many had been turned into solid bricks, their ancient pages glued together by the floods of water.

As the world woke up to the destruction of so many priceless art treasures, offers of assistance began pouring in to Italy. The difficulty for the authorities was that there was so much to restore, and so few experts available. Putting restoration projects on hold was not an option, they had to act quickly. For every day that passed, the damage became ever more ingrained.

It was decided to set up 'fast track' courses for students who could then be drafted in to work under the guidance of a professional supervisor. It was an exhaustive task. Each book, for instance, had to be carefully cleaned, dried, sprayed with fungicides and finally treated with chemicals to prevent the paper crumbling into dust. Every page had to be prised apart by hand. It was not a job for the nervous.

If the threat to Renaissance art treasures had gripped world attention, the people of northern Italy were more concerned with the every-day realities of life. Eight hundred districts had reported extensive damage. Around 22,000 farms and houses had been flooded, 100,000 cars, lorries and tractors saturated and 50,000 farm animals drowned or slaughtered. The national death toll was put at 112. The damage bill was £575 million.

Tuscans were assured that massive government aid was heading their way. They didn't count on it. Many years of experience had demonstrated to them how Italy's bureaucracy and endemic corruption could soak up public funds as effectively as a sponge on water. Quietly, families of the region got on with the task of rebuilding their homes themselves.

As Florence returned to normal, one question was fired again and again at city officials: 'What happens if the rain pours in this way again?'

The reply was not encouraging. 'We must just hope,' said a spokesman, 'that it won't.'

Aberfan

It seemed to have been raining forever in the Welsh valleys that autumn. Day after dismal day the grey clouds rolled in to saturate the earth, turning every playing field into a mud-bath and every mountain road into a fast-flowing stream. Even the hardy locals, used to coping with the worst of weathers, began to pray for a decent spell of sunshine.

The morning of 21 October 1966 was no different. A low mist swept along the valleys, its monotonous drizzle occasionally broken by light rain. In the little coal mining village of Aberfan, early risers turned up their coat collars as they trudged the streets. It was just another dreary, depressing day.

Except this day would be different. Today a black, slimy, suffocating, murderous monster would descend from the hills to destroy the heart of Aberfan, claiming its most precious assets – its children. No disaster has ever had quite the same effect on the British people. Just as many people can remember where they first heard of John F. Kennedy's assassination, so too they can recall the moment news came through about Aberfan.

At 7.30 am high above the village a giant slag heap known to the National Coal Board as Tip

Number 7 began to move. Imperceptibly at first, just a few trickles of slurry slipping down the hillside, but steadily gathering pace. Inch by inch, yard by yard, it rolled, lubricated by the rains and the oily, greasy mud which made up its 100,000-tonne mass. Soon nothing would stand in its way.

At 9.25 am the slurry avalanche crashed into Pantglas infants school and the row of cottages which stood alongside. Eye witnesses later recalled the terrible grinding and screeching of breaking rocks and wood, of splintering glass and of the first, awful screams of the victims inside.

One of those witnesses was the Rev. Kenneth Hayes. He strode around the corner of a village street to see a wall of slurry rising over the school, moulding itself around the building and then submerging it. He ran forward in disbelief, responding to a futile impulse to stop the mudslide with his bare hands. His nine-year-old son Dyfig was inside the school. Later he would identify the boy's body as it lay in a makeshift mortuary at Morriah Chapel.

'The slurry just overwhelmed the school,' he said. 'I saw the last of the living being taken out and the first of the dead. I knew I had lost my boy, although his body was not found until the following day. That was when the enormity of it all dawned on us. Whole families had been wiped out. I buried five from one house.'

Aberfan, 1966. Slag heaps, the land-scarring by-product of coal mining, tower ominously above Aberfan just two months before disaster struck.

A house engulfed by the slag heap that killed 144 people.

Inside the school the difference between life and death depended on which room staff and pupils were using. Those whose classes faced the slag heap bore the brunt of its destructive force. Those further away had a few precious seconds of warning which gave them time to avoid the inevitability of suffocation.

One of the fortunate ones was eight-year-old Pat Lewis. She stared open-mouthed at the wall splitting open behind her teacher as he called the register. Then she screamed and the warning was enough to get Pat and most of her class outside to safety. Her elder sister Sharon was not so lucky.

A terrified Pat ran back home where she fell into the arms of her mother, Sheila. Her first words were a mumbled apology: 'I've left my coat in school mam, sorry.' Then the tears poured out as she told what had happened. Grimly her mother, a trained nurse, swept Pat into her arms and ran to the school. There, climbing through a broken window, she saw a piteous sight.

'Inside were about twenty children who had been swept forward by the tip as it bulldozed the building,' she said. 'They were the ones who could be helped, though one of those children walked out of the ruins, seemingly all right, then collapsed and died.

'I laid the survivors on blankets in the school yard and turned the infants' classroom into a first aid post. I worked the whole day but nobody came out alive after 11 am. It was the most horrifying day, but your senses sharpen at times like that and so I can remember it all clearly.

'I knew I couldn't go and identify Sharon's body. My poor husband had to go and do it. He came back from the chapel at about 5 am on Saturday and said he recognised her. She had been found with the rest of the class and the teacher. I was sitting on a stool by the fire and I remember I slid back against the wall and made a terrible noise for I don't know how long.'

Some of the children escaped through a simple twist of fate. Young Phillip Thomas had just walked outside with a classmate to perform an errand for his teacher. When the mudslide arrived he was carried along on top of it rather than buried inside the school. His clearest memory is the pain of the rocks sandwiching his hands as he cried for his mother.

'I was buried immediately and found myself crying,' he said. 'Then all I remember was men digging me out and muddy water was pouring, pouring all over me.'

'Robert, the other boy on the errand, was found two days later, dead. My right hand was crushed so badly I lost three fingers. My leg was injured, my pelvis fractured, my hair gone. I had bleeding internally and externally and they said I would have bled to death if the mud hadn't caked on me, forming a skin. The force of the mud was such that it smashed my spleen, which had to be removed, and ripped off an ear, which had to be sewn back on.'

Then there was five-year-old Elizabeth Jones, who had been allowed to leave her desk to take some dinner money along to the school secretary's office. She said:

'I only remember being engulfed in masonry and sludge. I was trapped in the school corridor for a long time with the body of a little boy beneath me and by the side of me. When they pulled me out I was still holding my shilling dinner money. I am sure that saved me and I still keep it as a lucky coin.

'Most of my memories have mercifully faded, when your mind luckily begins to think of other things. But I received severe internal injuries in the slide and as a result will never have children.'

Other survivors told how their teacher saw the looming, black mountain rearing above the school as he glanced out of the window. In desperation he ordered them to hide under their desks, a move which undoubtedly helped save some. The little ones thought their teacher had gone mad to be playing such games in class.

Within minutes of the disaster occurring, the whole of Aberfan was descending on the devastated school and its pitiful occupants. Professional rescuers – the fire, police and ambulance service – found scores of willing hands to help them dig. Whether they were doctors or dustmen, teenagers or pensioners, the appalling scenes unfolding before their eyes united them in grief and exposed hidden strengths.

Off-duty miners, the sweat on their rock-hard muscles glistening like the tears in their eyes, tore into the slurry with a controlled madness. Perhaps they, more than any present, saw the terrible irony of what had happened. It was they who had toiled beneath the ground to produce coal and dump the unwanted slag. Now the industry which was their life, and helped them raise families, had robbed them of their children.

Throughout the rest of the day the rescue teams worked, calling for silence every so often in the hope of hearing a muffled cry of help. Darkness fell but the labours of the rescue services continued under the glare of powerful sodium lights. And one by one exhausted fathers were gently led away to their beds for a night in which sleep could never come.

Everyone spoke openly of their grief, and of cruelly dashed hopes. Mineworker Bryan Carpenter, who had been recovering in hospital after a pit accident, was brought to the school seeking news of his ten-year-old boy Desmond.

He said: 'When they told us of an unidentified ten-year-old in hospital our spirits lifted, but it turned out to be someone else. Later that night they found Desmond's body. We were by no means alone in our grief. In my street alone we lost fourteen. Two houses lost two children each. And time doesn't heal – there is always something there to trigger grief again.'

The final death toll that dreadful day was 144, of whom 116 were schoolchildren. They were buried on a hillside above the cemetery, around a giant cross of flowers laid out by mourners. The world shared the grief of Aberfan.

In 1967 a five-month official inquiry, involving 136 witnesses, concluded that Aberfan need never have happened. The National Coal Board had no clear national policy for safety standards at its slag heaps. Worse, the industry had received warnings from mining engineers that the Aberfan tip was unstable and unpredictable. For six years those warnings went unheeded.

Later the former NCB chairman Lord Robens summed up his feelings thus:

'The one question I constantly turn over in my mind is how it could have been prevented. There were thousands of pit heaps all over the country and they all came within the local pit authority's guidelines.'

'It is awful that it takes something like that to

make sure every safety regulation is double-checked and brought into practice.'

'When I think of all I did during my time with the Coal Board it diminishes to nothing when I think of the Aberfan disaster. It is a terrible thing which will always haunt me.'

For the still-grieving families there remains one unanswered question from the Aberfan tragedy. One of the lifeless little bodies pulled from the sludge was that of five-year-old Paul Davies. He had been busy drawing as the lethal slurry wall rolled unseen down the mountainside, right to the moment it hit the school. The pictures showed a mudslide engulfing the school while a plane with the markings 'National Coal Board' dropped bombs on the hill above. The picture also showed several clockfaces bearing the time 9.25. They pulled Paul and his pictures out from underneath the school clock. Its hands were stuck – at 9.25.

The Space Race

It was the biggest day in Christa McAuliffe's short life. Selected from more than 11,000 schoolteachers, she had been chosen by NASA to be the first civilian in space. Her brief was to teach two fifteen-minute lessons from the space shuttle *Challenger* as it orbited around the earth. Across America millions of children would tune in to her words via closed-circuit television.

On the morning of 28 January 1986, the seven astronauts entered their craft on the launchpad of Cape Canaveral and began the exhaustive task of checking all systems through the on-board computer. Commander Dick Scobee and pilot Michael Smith were strapped in to the front of the flight deck. Behind them sat electrical engineer Judith Resnik and physicist Ronald McNair. Below on the mid-deck were Greg Jarvis, another electrical engineer, Ellison Onizuka, an aerospace expert, and Christa.

NASA's 'ice team' – scientists responsible for spotting ice build up on the exterior of the shuttle and the booster rockets – had already given the spacecraft a thorough examination. Officials had sent them out three times since dawn, concerned that freezing temperatures the previous night could cause problems. The main worry was that

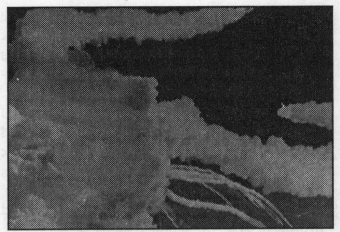

Cape Canaveral, 1986. Space shuttle *Challenger* explodes just 73 seconds into its flight. The seven astronauts were conscious for much of the cockpit's free-fall into the sea – dying instantly on impact.

The crew of *Apollo Fifteen*. In 1971 they erected a plaque on the moon honouring the eight astronauts and six cosmonauts who died during the first ten years of manned space exploration.

ice might break off during launch and damage *Challenger*'s heat resistant tiles. No one took much notice of an entry in one of the team's reports noting 'abnormal cold spots' on the right-hand booster rocket.

The on-board computer detected no internal malfunctions. At 'T' minus seven minutes and thirty seconds the walkway was winched back from the launchpad leaving the seven astronauts to make their final observations. Below them, 500,000 gallons of liquid oxygen and liquid hydrogen, and 1,000,000 pounds of solid fuel, was ready to feed the main engines. The atmosphere in the cockpit was typical of the 24 previous shuttle missions: calm efficiency tinged with a hint of tension.

Yet had the seven crew realised that an argument over safety was raging behind the scenes at NASA, it is doubtful any of them would have stepped aboard. A meeting had been called the previous evening between engineers from Morton Thiokol, the makers of the booster rockets, and NASA officials. The Thiokol people were worried about the cold weather and the effect it would have on the efficiency of rubber 'O-rings' used to seal joints in the four segments of the boosters. If the rings became too brittle they might fail to sit snugly and could allow exhaust gases to escape.

Thiokol's team stressed that below temperatures of 10°C the rings would be less supple. At Cape Canaveral the thermometers had dropped below freezing on the eve of launch. The engineers were unanimous. The flight would have to be delayed.

But NASA was having none of it. They had already postponed take-off three times since the original 25 January launch date. First a dust cloud hit the emergency landing area in Senegal, then rain at Cape Canaveral posed a threat to the heat-resistant tiles. A jammed bolt on an exterior hatch, and then strong winds, caused more delays. As discussions between NASA and Thiokol grew heated, one of the senior shuttle project officials asked: 'My God, when do you want me to launch? Next April?'

Allan McDonald, director in charge of the engineers, would still not give way. He refused to sign documentation giving official technical approval to the launch. 'I argued before and I argued after,' he later told journalists.

Eventually McDonald and his men were overruled when a senior vice-president at Morton Thiokol, Jerald Mason, explained that he had to 'make a management decision'. He and two other vice-presidents approved the launch as scheduled.

As countdown continued, the crowds massed around the Kennedy Space Center checked and re-checked their cameras. They knew the aims of the mission included launching a new communications satellite and monitoring Halley's Comet. Now they could follow the final moments before launch with the help of a NASA commentator.

As he announced 'T minus 45 seconds and counting' the excitement grew to fever pitch. Even though this was the 25th shuttle mission it still attracted huge interest among the American public. Besides, many close relatives of the astronauts were present in the VIP section of the public area.

Christa's family was standing with eighteen of her third-grade pupils. They had travelled the 1,500 miles from Concord, New Hampshire, to watch history in the making and now, as *Challenger*'s mighty engines roared into life, they craned their necks, desperate to get a good view.

'Four . . . three . . . two . . . one and lift off. Lift off of the 25th space shuttle mission. And it has cleared the tower.'

Smoothly, gracefully, *Challenger* rose through the clear skies rolling lazily onto her back as the computer selected a course to exit earth's atmosphere. At twenty seconds Mission Control said that all three engines were running smoothly.

'*Challenger*, go with throttle up,' instructed Mission Control, 52 seconds into the flight. 'Roger, go with throttle up,' Scobee replied.

Suddenly a dull orange glow emerged between the belly of the shuttle and one of the booster rockets. It was invisible to spectators on the ground but to observant TV viewers, taking advantage of NASA's powerful telescopic cameras, it was unmistakable. A moment later *Challenger* was in flames. Seventy three seconds into the flight she exploded.

The white plumes of smoke billowing crazily above Cape Canaveral stunned the crowd into silence. Then the scream of one woman was picked up by TV microphones. Her words were flashed around the world:

'Oh my God! What's happened?'

Cruelly, the launch commentator carried on as if nothing had happened. 'One minute, fifteen seconds,' he droned. 'Velocity 2900 feet per second. Altitude nine nautical miles. Down range distance seven nautical miles.' He was not looking at a TV screen but programmed flight data for what should have been the shuttle's progress.

Eventually the unreal monologue was halted. A full minute passed before the horrified and weeping crowds heard the loudspeakers again crackle to life:

'We have a report from the flight dynamics officer that the vehicle has exploded. The flight director confirms that.'

Minutes later the news was relayed to

Washington. Vice-president George Bush and White House Director of Communications Pat Buchanan rushed into the Oval Office where President Reagan was working. Buchanan knew there was no point breaking it gently. 'Sir,' he said, 'the shuttle has exploded'.

It had been Reagan's idea to make the first civilian in space a schoolteacher and he was devastated. His first question was to ask if any crew member had survived, but the eyes of his aides already told him the awful truth. In fact, NASA would later grudgingly reveal, the crew survived the initial explosion and were conscious for much of the cockpit's free-fall back to the surface. They died instantly when they hit the sea.

A few hours later, Reagan made one of his most powerful speeches to a nation in shock. Development of the shuttle had convinced most Americans that space travel was safe and reliable. More than that, it had become a symbol of their country's standing in the world.

Reagan told his national audience how the seven astronauts aboard *Challenger* had 'left the surly bonds of earth to touch the face of God'. Then, in a poignant address aimed specifically at children, he went on:

'I know it's hard to understand that sometimes painful things like this happen. It's all part of the process of exploration and expanding man's

Spectators in the VIP enclosure look on horrified as
Challenger **bursts into flames.**

horizons.' None felt it harder than Christa McAuliffe's pupils. For months after, they needed counselling for varying degrees of post-traumatic stress disorder.

Four days after the accident Reagan continued his theme at a memorial for the seven dead in front of six thousand NASA employees, selected politicians and the bereaved. Turning to the families of the astronauts he told them:

'The sacrifice of your loved ones has stirred the soul of our nation and, through the pain, our hearts have been opened to a profound truth: the future is not free. Dick, Mike, Judy, El, Ron, Greg and Christa, your families and your country mourn your passing. We bid you good-bye, but we will never forget you.'

It was the end of a defining week in Reagan's presidency. So much of his political agenda had rested on the shuttle's success. His dream of a 'star wars' defensive network, in which laser-equipped satellites would shoot down Soviet missiles in space, relied on NASA to put the hardware in orbit. Suddenly, the agency's ability to perform this task was under question.

In the weeks ahead, the US Coast Guard and NASA recovered amazingly large shuttle fragments from the Atlantic seabed. Despite the power of the explosion, some sections of the shattered fuselage were 25 feet long and the cabin containing the bodies was found intact. Each shuttle part was methodically logged to help investigators pinpoint the cause of the tragedy.

Of that there was little doubt. At least one of the quarter-inch thick, 37 feet long, O-rings had begun to burn soon after takeoff, igniting the highly-combustible gases in the right booster rocket. It was the same booster on which NASA's ice team had recorded abnormal cold spots on the morning of the launch. The engineers had been right to worry.

A Senate sub-committee later avoided pinning blame for the disaster on any named individuals. But it noted 'a serious flaw in the decision-making process' and submitted a 285-page report calling for a major re-design of key shuttle technology. NASA took note. By the time the next shuttle, *Discovery*, took off 32 months later, technicians had made 210 changes to the craft itself and 100 improvements to its computer software.

While defence and space budgets were a priority in the Reagan years, under President Clinton they have quickly taken a back seat. As the shuttle programme moves towards the new millennium its future looks precarious. Only time will tell if those seven brave astronauts lost their lives needlessly.

The disaster of *Challenger* was not the first of its kind . . .

The space race of the 1960s was supposed to be a voyage of discovery for humankind. In fact it was as much to do with superpower prestige as it was scientific progress. From the moment on 12 April 1961 that the Soviet Union succeeded in making Yuri Gagarin the first man in space, the United States and the Soviet Union were plunged into a new facet of the Cold War. Both nations wanted to show the world that their technology was best. The problem for Washington was that the Soviets had made all the running.

The announcement by President John F. Kennedy that the United States would put a man on the moon by the end of the decade changed everything. Virtually overnight, the Florida-based National Aeronautics and Space Administration (NASA) found itself with an open cheque book. The *Apollo* project was born, dedicated to humankind's first moonshot. During the mid-sixties film footage of yet another NASA spacecraft blasting off from the Kennedy Space Center became a familiar feature of worldwide TV news bulletins.

It was not until 1967 that the first *Apollo* rockets were ready. Up until now, spaceships were the safest form of travel known. Dozens of US astronauts and Soviet cosmonauts had gone into earth orbit, conducted space walks, and carried out gravity-free experiments. Each time they returned to earth safely, their capsules strung beneath nylon parachutes. But it was only a matter of time before something went wrong.

To the watching public, it all seemed as easy as catching a holiday flight. Unlike the scientists and officials at NASA, people couldn't easily comprehend the awesome power that was needed to escape the pull of earth's gravity. Besides they had a touching faith in American technology. The law of probability, which held that soon something would go wrong, was strictly for gloom and doom merchants.

Yet not even the most pessimistic space pundit could have predicted how the run of success would end. Kennedy's dream, borne so proudly by *Apollo One*, was cruelly shattered before the rocket even left the ground. The first disaster in the history of space exploration was caused by nothing more complicated than a loose wire.

For years NASA had been pondering how to save weight aboard its rockets, so making the task of the launch engines easier. One way was to use an atmosphere of pure oxygen inside the capsule.

Oxygen makes up one fifth of our air, the remainder being mostly nitrogen. This atmospheric mixture was used in Soviet spacecraft, even though it meant bolting in heavy, cumbersome nitrogen and oxygen cylinders along with equipment to mix the two gases safely. The

Soviets had little need to worry about the extra weight carried. Their giant *Proton* booster rockets were easily capable of producing the required thrust. They feared that oxygen on its own was too combustible.

NASA acknowledged that its *Apollo* rockets were less powerful but claimed the use of pure oxygen would significantly ease their payload. As to the fire danger, scientists at the manned Spacecraft center in Houston, Texas, came up with some reassuring arguments.

The reason fire spread, they observed, was because oxygen heated by a flame rises up pulling in fresh, cold oxygen behind it. This intake feeds the blaze and so assists it to expand.

But in space, the Houston team explained, there was no gravity and no up or down. Even if oxygen did ignite, it could not rise in the heat. It would simply smother itself.

Others were not so confident. Two years before *Apollo One* was due to blast off, NASA's senior medical advisor, Dr Randolph Lovelace, specifically warned the Agency about 'the potential dangers of 100 per cent oxygen atmosphere'. He told how in one experiment, involving a space capsule carried inside an aeroplane at 33,000 feet, the tube in a television monitor overheated and dripped molten plastic onto a control panel. The crew smelt the fumes and were able to extinguish the fire.

But, Dr Lovelace argued: 'Instead of focusing attention on the hazards of fire, this accident gave a false sense of security.'

He also drew attention to a blaze inside a capsule simulator at the Brooks Air Force Base, Texas. Two crew in full space suits noticed a dull glow behind an instrument console. Within seconds the console was in flames.

The most serious fire of all was recorded at Philadelphia's Naval Air Center inside an oxygen chamber pressurised to within only a third of the levels planned for Apollo. One of four crewmen working in the chamber caused a minute spark as he tried to change an electric light bulb. A flash fire instantly erupted, setting fire to the men's clothes and inflicting appalling burns on them.

NASA could not say it was never warned. Yet by 1967 the project was already too far advanced to make wholesale changes. If Kennedy's challenge was to be answered, the use of pure oxygen could no longer be the subject of debate. Besides, the Soviets were rumoured to be attempting a moonshot. In Kennedy's honour, America had to get in first.

The man selected to command the *Apollo One* mission was Gus Grissom, certainly no stranger to danger. The Korean war ace had made two previous space flights, the first of which he was extremely lucky to survive. Grissom's *Mercury* spacecraft splashed down safely in the Pacific only for the impact to dislodge his escape hatch. Helpless, he had an agonising wait in his sinking capsule before NASA divers eventually managed to get him out.

A few weeks before the *Apollo One* mission, Grissom attended a hearing of the US Congressional Space Committee. With him was another senior astronaut John Glenn. Grissom nodded enthusiastically as he heard Glenn's blunt words to the congressmen:

'You may as well realise now that some future space flights will fail, probably with the loss of life. There will be failures, there will be sacrifices, there will be times when we are not riding on such a crest of happiness as we are now.'

On 27 January 1967, 40-year-old Grissom reported to Launch Pad 34 at the Kennedy Space Center. With him were fellow crew members Roger Chaffee, 31, a naval lieutenant commander eager to begin his debut mission, and the veteran space walker Ed White, 36.

Although *Apollo One*'s launch date was still a month away, the three had to practice and hone their cockpit drill. That meant strapping themselves in to the command module for five-hour stretches at a time, lying uncomfortably on their backs in full space suits. Time and again the men would run through the drill, Grissom giving standard, clipped responses to ground control's requests for the information displayed by his on-board computer.

Like the astronauts, NASA technicians manning ground control's vast bank of monitors found the practice runs rather tedious. The format rarely changed. There was little to do except watch and wait.

Suddenly one technician saw his TV screen flash white and then darken. Irritated, he leaned forward to twiddle the brightness and contrast controls. Somehow his link to a camera inside the capsule had been broken.

A split second later an agonised yell sounded over the intercom link: 'Fire . . . I smell fire.' There were three seconds of silence before Ed White's desperate voice confirmed: 'Fire in the cockpit!'

Then came the dreadful sound of the doomed astronauts pounding and clawing at the escape hatch. Seven seconds later Roger Chaffee screamed: 'We're on fire. Get us outa here.' Then nothing but silence.

It took 4 minutes for a rescue team to get from their blastproof base to the top of the 218 feet launch tower. Sprinting out of the high-speed elevator two of them grabbed *Apollo One*'s escape hatch handles, ignoring the heat which seared through their gloves. It was already too late. All three men had died in seconds from the inferno that engulfed them. Their bodies remained strapped in their seats within the heat-resistant spacesuits.

As flames roared out of the command module the rescue team was forced back. All power to the spacecraft was cut and launch director Dr Kurt Dubus ordered the men on the tower: 'Stay away from the capsule. There is nothing you can do for them now.'

For six despairing hours the bodies stayed in place – clearly visible on the ground control monitors. Many of the technicians cried openly. Few could bear to look at their dead colleagues. Eventually, Debus decided the danger of an explosion had passed and permitted rescuers to recover the corpses. At midnight they were gently carried out of the scorched cockpit.

Later investigations pinpointed the cause of the fire as a loose wire behind the control panel. Had the capsule's atmosphere been an oxygen-nitrogen mix, it would almost certainly extinguished itself. In pure oxygen it sparked certain death.

NASA, however, refused to change tack. The *Apollo* programme was set back eighteen months while spark-proof electrical circuitry was fitted along with a quick-release space hatch. A year after these refinements were implemented, on 21

July 1969, *Apollo Eleven* put Neil Armstrong's lunar module on the moon and John F. Kennedy's American dream was fulfilled.

Once America had won the race to the moon the Soviets decided to counter with another first. On 19 April 1971 they put the world's first permanent space station, *Salyut One*, into orbit. Then, on 6 June, cosmonauts aboard the *Soyuz Eleven* rocket managed to dock safely with the *Salyut* and crawled inside to begin what would be a record spell in space of 23 days.

The three cosmonauts, commander Georgi Dobrovolsky, 43, test engineer Viktor Patsayev, 38, and flight engineer Vladislav Volkov, completed a flawless mission. One of the most interesting aspects as far as ground-based Soviet scientists were concerned was to establish how well their bodies would cope with the effects of weightlessness. In zero gravity their muscles would not need to work hard as on earth and would waste away.

As the three men began their slow descent home, excited ground controllers reminded them not to try to leave their capsule on landing. Once they were safely on the ground they would have to be carried out by medical teams. Dobrovolsky laughed at this. 'Don't worry, we will just sit back and let you do all the work,' he replied.

At 23,000 feet *Soyuz Eleven* released its

parachutes to begin the gentle glide to earth. As usual, radio contact had been lost in the scorching heat of re-entry to the atmosphere. It was never regained. A recovery team was about to find out why.

As *Soyuz* fired her retro engines for a final time to negotiate a perfect landing, medics rushed forward to carry the nation's heroes into helicopters stationed close by. When they opened the main hatch they witnessed a terrible sight.

All three cosmonauts were dead.

It seems explosive charges used to disengage *Soyuz* from *Salyut* had knocked open a valve in the hatch. Throughout its trip home, *Soyuz* had been leaking air into space. By the time Dobrovolsky realised what was going on the huge forces of atmospheric deceleration, combined with his own muscle weakness, meant he could not even lift an arm to shut the valve. All three men had to sit and wait for death to come.

Despite the intense rivalry, the political rhetoric and the national pride that became synonymous with the space race, both sides were united in grief at disasters such as *Apollo One* and *Soyuz Eleven*.

On 30 July 1971 *Apollo Fifteen* astronauts David Scott and Jim Irwin touched down on the moon with their sophisticated battery-powered car, the *Lunar Rover*. During one of their excursions they drove to the edge of a massive chasm, the Hadley Rille, below a 400 metre high cliff. There they gently placed a small metal sculpture of a fallen spaceman and a plaque listing the names, in alphabetical order, of the eight astronauts and six cosmonauts who gave their lives during the first ten years of manned space exploration. The plaque made no mention of the men's nationalities.

Seveso

The scene in the little northern Italian town of Seveso could have been culled straight from a 1950s science-fiction movie. One moment it was just another quiet, sultry Saturday afternoon. The next there was mayhem. Families sitting at pavement cafes began choking. Children playing football in the street started screaming with pain. Birds dropped down dead out of the sky. It was as though a silent, invisible killer had been unleashed.

Only a few men could hazard a guess as to the cause. Shortly after lunch that day – 10 July 1976 – weekend workers at a local chemical company heard a loud bang followed by a strange whistling sound. They ran outside to find a chemical reactor spewing a fine white dust cloud from a safety valve.

The men on duty quickly opened up water pipes into the reactor, flooding it to prevent further contamination. But the process took several minutes. By that time the cloud was floating inexorably through Seveso and other villages of the beautiful Po valley, sparing no one within an area of six square miles.

The chemical deposited was dioxin, one of the deadliest poisons known to humankind. It is

Italy, 1976. An unseen but deadly dioxin gas leakage enveloped the town of Seveso. A guard prevents anyone entering the quarantined area.

Scientists wearing protective clothing take soil samples to gauge the concentration of the poisoning.

thought less than four ounces in water supplies would be sufficient to kill everyone in a city the size of London. In the skies above Seveso that summer's day, there was enough concentrated dioxin to wipe out one-third of the entire American population.

The chemical factory was run by Swiss-based Icmesa, itself part of the multinational Hoffman-La Roche pharmaceutical company. It manufactured trichlorophenol for use in domestic cleaners, soap and anti-perspirants. One of the by-products of the process was dioxin gas.

Normally factories such as this are equipped with huge dump tanks which act as a back-up for when gas is released through safety valves. The tanks are equipped to absorb toxic fumes and clean them up for safe release into the atmosphere. The 160 employees of Icmesa in Seveso had nothing as sophisticated to hand.

It was not difficult to work out what had gone wrong. A chemical process carried out in the reactor the previous day had failed to cool properly and the residual heat influenced the reaction which followed. Icmesa's senior management were made aware of what happened but, initially at least, they kept the knowledge to themselves. Perhaps they hoped the dioxin escape would pass off relatively unnoticed. If so, they could not have made a worse misjudgement.

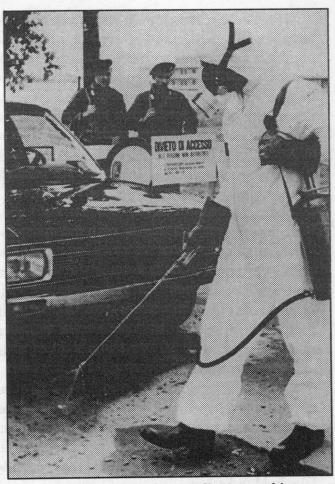

To prevent contamination spreading, everything
leaving the quarantined area had to be disinfected.

Over the next few days thousands of pets and farm animals died, crops started to wither and hundreds of people presented themselves to hospitals suffering from vomiting, headaches and blurred vision. Soon, worse side-effects appeared in the form of a painful and unsightly skin disease called chloracne. Others suffered skin rashes and pus-boils, even backache. All told how the air last Saturday afternoon was heavy with the acrid odour of burning plastic.

Doctors were baffled by the phenomenon and were unsure what treatment to use. It seemed no family among the 17,000 residents of Seveso had been left unscathed and more casualties were coming forward each day. Livestock and wildlife seemed to have been particularly badly hit. Farmers found herds of cows bleeding from their ears and eyes, whole chicken roosts wiped out and crops which seemed to have been scorched.

Cats and dogs would suddenly keel over in the street, their fly-covered carcasses left stinking in the sun. One man told how he saw three robins hopping in his garden suddenly drop dead. As the week rolled on, an air of panic and fear began to take hold in Seveso.

The main cause of that panic was lack of information. Because there had been no obvious disaster, such as a blaze or explosion, in any of the local factories, the authorities were unsure which way to turn. The media response was also muted. No TV stations or national newspapers had got to grips with the story. Icmesa itself saw no reason to make a statement.

On Friday, all that changed. A two-year-old child was rushed to hospital with her body a putrid mass of boils and blisters. Doctors who were already highly suspicious of Icmesa's role in the tragedy now lost patience and demanded some straight answers. The mayors of both Seveso and the nearby town of Meda began making threatening noises.

Icmesa offered only a bland, non-committal response. Soil samples, they said, were being analysed by scientists in Switzerland. In the meantime they advised that posters should be put up around town warning the public not to eat locally-grown produce.

That same night, another eighteen children were brought into hospital. With every hour that passed it seemed the effects of the poison cloud were becoming more prevalent. Yet medical staff could not understand why treatment seemed so ineffective. The advice from Icmesa was that patients had probably been exposed to a dose of the skin irritant trichlorophenol, or TCP.

It is not surprising the doctors felt their skills were impotent. TCP is roughly one million times less toxic than dioxin. As one biochemist put it later: 'It was a bit like prescribing aspirin for a patient complaining of headaches and then discovering he had a brain tumour all along.'

By now the media had cottoned on to what was fast becoming Italy's most insidious disaster. Reporter Bruno Ambrosi, based just thirteen miles from Seveso in Milan, remembered a few snippets from student science lectures and decided to check out the chemical make-up of TCP. Sure enough, he unearthed a vital clue. If TCP was heated above 200°C it gave off dioxin.

Ambrosi then discovered how dioxin could destroy tissue such as the liver and kidneys, how it could mutate chromosomes to induce cancers and how unborn children ran the risk of being born deformed. One paragraph from an academic paper sprang out at him:

'It is the most potent small-molecule toxin known to man. Its effects dwarf those of arsenic and strychnine.'

Ambrosi's story was published just as the Swiss scientists confirmed that soil around Seveso contained huge quantities of dioxin. They pointed out that it would not disperse in water and could potentially contaminate the landscape for many years. The Italian government responded by declaring a state of emergency.

On 24 July an evacuation began from the worst affected area of Seveso. Once the 200 families had left, squads of police and caribinieri threw a cordon around their homes reinforced by six miles of barbed wire. Then a team dressed in charcoal-lined protective suits moved systematically through the zone slaughtering every living thing they could find. Most were already close to death.

When it was over, more than 60,000 animal corpses lay piled haphazardly in fields and streets. No wonder Seveso was quickly nicknamed the 'Dead Zone'.

The aftermath of the disaster proved to be an unprecedented public health hazard. Thousands of tonnes of soil were removed and encased in concrete. Contaminated plants and carcasses were burnt. More than 250 people had to be re-housed. Yet the worst fear of all was the effect dioxin could have on future generations. Despite frowns of disapproval from some in the Catholic Church, the Italian government declared that abortions throughout the area would be made temporarily legal.

Incredibly, not a single person is yet known to have died as a result of exposure to the toxic cloud. And of the 190 children who suffered from chloracne, all but two made a full recovery.

In 1979 a government inquiry into the Seveso disaster delivered a withering condemnation of Icmesa. It accused factory bosses of using unsafe equipment and expressed disbelief that they had waited 27 hours before informing a low-ranking town hall official of the dioxin danger. Later, Icmesa was forced to hand out compensation cheques totalling £8 million.

Today it remains unclear whether exposure to the chemical will rebound on the next generation of babies. Genetic mutations can sometimes emerge after many years of lying dormant in a particular family. For the residents of Seveso, only time will tell.

The Tenerife Air Crash

It had never happened before and, thankfully, nothing quite like it has ever happened since. It was the nightmare of every airline, every pilot, every air traffic controller – and of every flying passenger. This ultimate horror was the collision between two jumbo jets laden with passengers and it happened on the runway of Los Rodeos Airport, Santa Cruz, on the Atlantic island of Tenerife on 27 March 1977.

It was a Sunday, always a busy time on the holiday isle. On this day, however, there was additional chaos, confusion and fear. A terrorist bomb had exploded in a shop at Las Palmas Airport on the neighbouring Spanish-administered island of Gran Canaria, with the telephoned threat that a second bomb attack was planned for later.

The blast killed no one and the second bomb never materialised. But the perpetrators of the attack never realised what terrible carnage their cowardly actions would ultimately cause.

Aircraft heading for Gran Canaria were diverted to Tenerife, already encountering handling problems because of thick fog – not unusual for the tiny island, where clouds build up around the extinct volcano of Mount Teide.

Among the diverted aircraft were two Boeing 747 jumbo jets: Dutch KLM flight 4805 from Amsterdam and Pan American flight 1736 from Los Angeles and New York.

Now, as the afternoon wore on, the flight crew of both aircraft received the welcome news that Las Palmas airport had now been cleared for landing. At last they were on their way to their rightful destination.

Pan Am pilot Victor Grubbs was carefully taxiing his fully-loaded 747 along the runway at Los Rodeos awaiting permission from the control tower to take off. Soon he and his 380 passengers, mostly vacationers from California on their way to rendezvous with an American cruise ship, would be on their way towards the blue skies beyond the clammy fog bank.

Captain Victor Grubbs was an ultra-cautious old-stage whose safety record with Pan American was immaculate. Aboard the KLM jumbo jet, somewhere out of sight across the foggy runway, sat his counterpart, Captain Jaap van Zanten, peering anxiously through the flightdeck windows as he, too, taxied carefully around the peripheral runways.

Captain van Zanten was also a long-serving pilot; he had been with KLM for 27 years and had appeared in the airlines advertisements to underline their expertise and their safety record.

In his safe hands that day were 229 Dutch passengers who had also been bound for Las Palmas before their flight had been diverted because of the bomb.

By now visibility was down to 500 yards – low but still within the permitted limits for take-off. Because of the congestion around the airport, both pilots Grubbs and van Zanten were ordered by the control tower to taxi their respective airplanes up the main runway to the take-off starting point at the far end.

Captain van Zanten heard the control tower tell him: Flight 4805 taxi straight ahead to the end of the runway and make backtrack.

The jumbo completed this manoeuvre and the co-pilot reported: 'KLM is now ready for take-off; we are waiting for clearance.'

The tower replied: 'OK, stand by for take-off; I will call you.'

The Pan Am jumbo, meanwhile, was receiving instructions to taxi up the runway behind the KLM jet – but to turn off by one of the exits on the left, thus leaving the main runway free for the KLM flight to take off.

Controllers asked Pan Am Captain Grubbs whether he had completed his turn-off, and when he replied that he had not yet done so, they then instructed him: 'Do so and advise when the runway is clear.'

Then came a further message from the KLM jumbo to the tower. It relayed routine advice about the projected path once it had left the airport, and ended indistinctly with the words: 'We are now ready on (or 'at') take-off.'

But Captain Grubbs, his plane, his crew and his 380 passengers were still on the main runway pointing straight through the mist at Captain van Zanten and the invisible KLM jumbo.

It was just before 6.30 pm that the nightmare became reality. Grubbs could scarcely believe his eyes as the lights of the KLM jet emerged through the fog.

At first he thought the mist must be lifting and the jumbo ahead of him was in fact stationary. Then, as the lights grew brighter and closer, the awful truth dawned – the Dutch aircraft was bearing down on him at take-off speed of 160 miles per hour.

Grubbs screamed into his headset: 'There he is! . . . Look at him . . . That . . . that . . . son of a bitch is coming!'

His co-pilot, Robert Bragg, yelled: 'Get off! Get off!'

Captain van Zanten was by now also aware of the disaster looming. He watched the Pan Am plane slewing round in front of him in a vain attempt to get off the runway and out of his path. But his plane's speed was by now so high that the

Dutchman could not stop. His KLM aircraft had reached the point of no return. The two planes would undoubtedly collide.

The Dutch pilot desperately wrestled with the controls to make the KLM jumbo lift off from the runway early – in effect, hopping over the Pan Am plane in front of him. But he was too late. The nose lifted but the tail remained on the runway, digging a trench in the tarmac. Two seconds later, the bottom of KLM 4805 hit the top of Pan Am 1736.

The belly of the KLM aeroplane smashed into the forward part of the Pan Am air craft's second-class section, while the left wing sliced off the roof and bubble of the cockpit. Pan Am 4805 was cut in half. Blazing, the aeroplane collapsed onto the side of the runway.

Aboard the American plane there was confusion. Some passengers fell burning to the ground. The luckier ones picked themselves up and dazedly stumbled to safety. Others were too stunned to move and were consumed by the flames where they sat rooted to their seats. The air hissed with death screams.

Meanwhile, the Dutch plane had slammed back onto the runway, skidded around in a circle and come to a suddering halt 300 yards down the runway. There was a moment's stillness. Then it exploded in a massive fireball, the inferno gorging on itself and on the freshly-filled fuel tanks. Steel and aluminium vaporised.

All 248 people aboard the KLM plane were killed instantly.

Of the 396 passengers and crew of the Pan Am jumbo, only 70 escaped from the wreckage, and nine of them died later in hospital. A total of 583 people lost their lives that Sunday evening in possibly the worst disaster in aviation history.

The Atlantic Empress

For years it had been an environmentalist's nightmare. The prospect of two giant oil tankers colliding at speed in mid-ocean was unthinkable, both in terms of the risk to crews and the effect on marine life. Some said modern equipment made such a catastrophe impossible. They forgot the first principle of 'Sod's Law' – if a system can go wrong, it will go wrong.

The collision of the 210,257-tonne Liberian-registered *Aegean Captain* and the 292,666-tonne Greek-flagged *Atlantic Empress* turned the nightmare into grim reality. The ships, known as VLCCs (Very Large Crude Carriers) in maritime jargon, carried a staggering 480,000 tonnes of oil between them and together produced the world's worst sea pollution incident involving tankers. These leviathans were also responsible for causing the destruction of the largest vessel ever lost in an accident at sea.

On 17 July 1979 the *Aegean Captain* left the port of Bonaire in the West Indies, fully loaded, en route to Singapore. At 5.10 pm on 19 July she logged to a position about 8 miles north of Little Tobago Island, before changing to a course of 122 degrees. She was under the control of an automatic pilot, making about 14 knots.

The Greek master, Captain Ionnis A. Zissakis, left the bridge at about 6.15 pm, leaving his chief officer in charge. The second mate and an able-bodied seaman were also on duty, the latter acting as lookout. At about 6.30 pm, this seaman was allowed to go below for his usual 30 minute coffee break.

There was a rain squall showing up as interference on the radar but the crew later claimed they could see no other 'targets' ahead. Within ten minutes, the rainstorm struck, reducing visibility to less than a mile.

It is less clear what was happening on the *Atlantic Empress*. The vessel was lost with all records in the disaster and Captain Paschalis Chatzipetros failed to attend either of the inquiry hearings that followed later. What is known is that the ship had just made landfall after a long voyage across the South Atlantic from the Cape of Good Hope. She was also without one of her three second officers. He had left during a port stopover in England during May and had not been replaced. Instead Captain Chatzipetros was using a short-sighted radio officer as an unqualified stand-in for the lookout rota.

This officer, according to several witnesses, had been drinking earlier in the day. For some unaccountable reason he sent the seaman on watch with him below for a break just as the

Empress entered the rain squall. As the Board of Investigation put it later:

'It is an arresting fact that a laden VLCC should be proceeding into the dusk in the charge of an uncertified watchkeeper, a radio officer who was being paid to double as a desk officer, who was known to be an habitual drunkard and who on this occasion was affected by alcohol recently taken, in the opinion of the able seaman who stood the watch with him.'

When Captain Chatzipetros arrived on the bridge at 7 pm, he immediately berated his radio man for allowing the seaman to leave. He didn't order the man to return, but in any case, it would have made no difference. Neither vessel had kept a proper radar check and the rain ruled out reliance on visual contact. Suddenly, out of the mist, the aghast Chatzipetros spotted the lights of the *Aegean Captain* bearing down on him. She was about a mile away and making fifteen knots.

At the speeds the two carriers were travelling, this distance might as well have been a couple of yards. It can take twenty miles to bring a tanker to a standstill and to manoeuvre one quickly in an emergency is quite impossible. At 7.04 pm the *Aegean Captain* struck the *Empress* on her port side at an angle of 30 degrees. The latter's number three wing tank burst into flames which then swept across the fore-deck of the *Aegean Captain*.

Fortunately for Zissakis, his ship was equipped with an IGS (Inert Gas System) in which fire-damping gases produced by the engines were pumped around the cargo hold to prevent ignition. The *Empress* had no such system and it cost her dear. While Zissakis got all but one of his men off safely, there were scenes of panic and chaos aboard Chatzipetros's vessel.

As fire raged from the ruptured tanks, the *Empress*'s crew flailed about trying to understand how the lifeboats worked. They had mistaken the bridge 'emergency signal' for the 'abandon ship' signal and as a result there were no officers present to supervise the launching of the boats.

The crew themselves had received only the briefest of induction courses. Weekly lifesaving drills, demanded by Greek law, had not been carried out for months. To make matters worse, no one had bothered to maintain the equipment with the result that when an attempt was made to set the boats free in the water, the release mechanisms failed. The tiny craft were then dragged along under the continuing motion of the tanker, shipping water all the time. Many of the occupants in the boats were drowned. Of the *Empress*'s 42 crew and passengers, 26 died.

The *Atlantic Empress* sank, discharging 265,000 tonnes of oil into the sea. Though the *Aegean Captains*' hull was also punctured she lost only 14,000 tonnes. Later she was towed into Curacao where the rest of her cargo was safely pumped off. The ship herself was declared an insurance write-off.

The effect on wildlife around the West Indies was incalculable. But many thousands of birds, and probably millions of fish, died as a result of the black tide that lapped for miles around the collision point. As ever, the world looked for someone to blame and the captains and crews of the tankers took the brunt of it.

Captain Zissakis was criticised for failing to instruct his watch officers in the performance of their duties. But he at least escaped with his master's certificate intact. Not so Captain Chatzipetros who, International Maritime Organisation investigators believed, had shown a total lack of managerial ability and failed to instil a sense of leadership. Chatzipetros's licence was duly revoked. The drunken radio officer was never called to answer for his actions. He perished in the sea.

The MGM Fire

They came to Las Vegas to try their luck and pocket a fortune. By nightfall on 21 November 1980 the gambling guests who survived the *Grand Hotel* fire had a new insight into luck. They were plain lucky to be alive.

That day the *Grand* turned into a real-life version of the disaster movie classic *Towering Inferno*. A fire which began in a pan of cooking oil engulfed the entire £50 million, 2,100 bedroom complex and claimed the lives of 84 people. It was one of the worst hotel fires in American history and it ended in law suits totalling almost US$2 billion against the owners, MGM Hotel Corporation.

Like Vegas itself, the *Grand* was big, bright and brash. It was named after MGM's Greta Garbo blockbuster of the 1930s and its managers prided themselves on a reputation for attracting international show business acts like Tom Jones and Englebert Humperdinck. Paying £125,000 a week to these stars was a bargain when considering the kudos that came with them. Big name singers seemed to pull in big money gamblers.

The previous year had been one of the most successful-ever for the state of Nevada's casino tycoons. Their predecessors had transformed

Vegas from a small town mining community of 8000 in 1905, into a thriving modern metropolis. A relaxed attitude to gambling by legislators was the secret of its success. In 1979 the combined gambling take across the state was put at a mind-boggling US$2.1 billion. Future turnover projections looked healthy.

At 7.15 am on the day of the *Grand* disaster the hotel was already teeming with people. In a city which boasts that it doesn't need clocks, many guests had been up all night playing the roulette and blackjack tables and pumping dollars into the 1000-plus fruit machines. With the chance to win $1 million for a $10 stake there was no time to waste.

In the huge basement kitchen, which produced meals for the hotel's five separate restaurants, the staff were gearing up for their busiest period. No one noticed the smoke curling lazily from a pan of cooking oil. Seconds later the oil ignited.

Instantly the ceiling was set alight and with frightening speed a fireball exploded through the stairwell and into the 50-metre long casino. Ten guests died before they could leave their seats. Others seemed rooted to the spot, staring dumbly at the holocaust unfolding before their eyes. Men in dinner suits shuffled nervously. Suddenly a woman swathed in furs and dripping with expensive jewellery screamed.

The casino staff moved first. Croupiers yanked out their cash drawers and raced for the fire exit. Security officers poured dollar bills into a nearby fireproof vault. Gradually the customers caught on to what was happening. Those still heavily under the influence of alcohol sobered up fast, crammed their betting chips into their jacket pockets and joined the exodus.

Around them the blaze intensified. A giant electronic scoreboard for Keno (a game similar to bingo) blew up creating a second fireball. Plastic furnishings melted, blazing droplets rained from the false ceiling setting off fountains of fire across the synthetic carpets. Now deadly noxious smoke filled the air asphyxiating anyone and everyone in its path. It was a scene which could have been conjured up by the Devil himself.

The rapid spread of the fire bewildered the terrified guests, yet it was no surprise to investigators who later inspected the charred rooms. There were massive holes along one side of the hotel where construction work was underway. These acted as a giant air intake, effectively turning the *Grand* into a giant furnace. Panicking hotel residents who smashed their way out through windows made matters worse.

Amazingly, there were hundreds of guests in the upper rooms who slept, blissfully unaware of the human tragedy unfolding beneath them. No alarm had been sounded because the central amplifier was destroyed before it could come to life. There were no smoke detectors, so the deadly fumes swirling along the corridors and lift shafts went largely unheeded. Some fire doors had been wedged open, allowing the blaze to progress quickly. Others were locked shut, condemning several people to a horrendous death.

Where the fire alarms failed, the sound of twelve US Air Force rescue helicopters succeeded. Guests dashed to the windows of their mirror-ceiling rooms to see who was causing the commotion. They heard the loud speakers exhorting them to climb to the top of the hotel where they could be winched to safety.

Now pandemonium broke out. People found they could not open their windows to suck fresh air because of special catches to thwart suicides. Others realised that the ladders of the 40 fire engines below extended only to the ninth floor.

The lucky ones managed to scramble down scaffolding or hitch a ride down in the *Grand*'s external window-cleaning lift. Others, driven to the edge of sanity by the merciless fumes hurled themselves to their deaths from rooms as high as the seventeenth floor. 'People were screaming and throwing furniture through windows,' said senior fire officer Ralph Dinsman. 'They were begging to be saved.'

Many of the survivors told extraordinary tales of daring and good fortune. British businessmen Roy Taylor and David McAllister were sharing a room together on the sixth floor of the hotel and only woke up because their bedside alarm sounded unexpectedly.

Mr Taylor said: 'We had forgotten to switch the clock off and it rang at 6.40 am. I turned it off and we were just going back to sleep when David mumbled about smelling something burning. We opened the bedroom door and were knocked back by a wall of smoke. We tried to open the window, but there were catches designed to stop people falling out. We hurled a coffee table through the glass and then dropped mattresses and bedding onto a flat roof 40 feet below. David hung by his hands from the sill, then dropped. I was about to do the same when he shouted, "Go back". I ducked as a shower of glass cascaded down from above. It would have sliced my head off. Then I jumped.'

Some other Britons, holidaymakers Russell and Lilian Ireland, from London, were up early to get ready for their flight home. Mr Ireland said: 'There were no alarms, no sprinklers, and no directions to the fire escapes. I grabbed Lilian and told two other women to follow us. The fire door was locked but we managed to tear the damn thing open. It was a hell of a difficult job.'

Greg Williams made his escape using a tip he remembered from the *Towering Inferno* movie. 'I'd seen the film,' he said, 'I wrapped a wet towel round my head, got down on my hands and knees and crawled under the smoke to a fire exit.'

Others were brought out alive from their rooms, even though they were convinced they were going to die. James Mackey and his wife, from Michigan, heard about the fire on a radio newsflash. Realising they were already too late to escape, they placed mattresses around the walls to insulate them from the heat and stuffed towels under the door to keep out fumes. 'We put a note on the door and prayed a lot,' was how Mr Mackey later summed up his survival tactics.

Sixty feet below them in another bedroom, Keith Breverton opened his door to what he later described as 'an impassable hell'.

'It was death, absolute death out there,' he said later. 'People were screaming 'What shall we do?'' Resigned to his fate Mr Breverton lay on the floor of his room and scribbled what he believed would be his last messages to friends and family. He was found unconscious by rescue workers but made a full recovery.

After two hours the first fireman entered the blackened building to begin the gruesome task of recovering bodies. It was easy to spot those who had died instantly. They included a waiter lying next to a tray on which he'd been serving breakfast and a gambler slumped underneath his seat at the roulette table.

There were also those for whom death had come agonisingly slowly. On one staircase eighteen asphyxiated bodies were found pathetically clinging together – they had been trapped between a deadly smoke cloud and a door that was jammed fast.

In the inquiry that followed Hotel president Bernard Rothkopf claimed the hotel had followed all fire safety codes. He was supported by an independent security expert, Don Busser, who added: 'You cannot blame MGM management entirely. The state bears some responsibility.' The *Grand*, he pointed out, had conformed to all the requirements in force when it was built in 1970. Tough new rules announced nine years later applied only to new buildings.

Throughout 1981 MGM shares took a battering on Wall Street as investors pondered what long-term effects the fire might have on the company's business. Las Vegas too suffered a backlash in the form of a $20 million drop in revenues in the first quarter. But MGM had no intention of being driven off the Strip. It responded by rebuilding the *Grand* to incorporate some of the most advanced fire safety technology in the world.

There was a $6 million computer-controlled fire detection system, an intercom direct to every suite to relay instructions from the hotel's major incident room, four sprinklers and a smoke detector in each bedroom, fans able to suck toxic fumes out of the building and doors which could all be opened simultaneously in an emergency. There was even an introductory five-minute video for new guests in which film legend Gene Kelly told them what to do in an emergency.

The total cost was $25 million, although it was a small price to pay to restore the *Grand*'s reputation. As every casino owner knows, luck is not enough to ensure survival. You need the odds in your favour.

The Potomac Air Crash

On 13 January 1982 blizzards swept in to Washington DC from the north-east, blanketing the city soon after sunrise. Throughout the morning the flakes fell steadily and many companies and government officials decided to allow staff home early. By mid-afternoon there was a five-inch covering in places. It was a long, slow crawl home on every highway on roads choked with traffic.

The city's National Airport was also caught by surprise. On the departures timetable most services were shown as delayed and Air Florida Flight 90, bound for Fort Lauderdale and Tampa, was no exception. It should have taken off at 2.15 pm but it was 3 pm before the 71 passengers were even moved out of the departure lounge.

On the flight deck Captain Larry Wheaton and co-pilot Roger Pettit gazed despondently out across the runway watching incoming planes taxi to their assigned satellites. Many of the aircraft had huge icicles hanging from their wings, a problem that could interfere with the aeroplane's handling. Pettit stared at the airport workmen trying to de-ice the wings of the Air Florida Boeing 737. It made him feel uncomfortable.

'Boy this is a losing battle trying to de-ice those

things,' he said. 'It gives you a false feeling of security and that's all it does.'

Captain Wheaton also seemed gloomy. 'I'm certainly glad there's people taxiing on the same place I want to go,' he said. 'I can't see the runway without these flags. Maybe further up.'

Head stewardess Donna Adams was less concerned. She had total faith in the men flying the 737 and she had few worries about the problems the weather might cause them. 'I love it out here,' she said. 'Look at all the tyre tracks in the snow.'

At 3.58 pm air traffic control gave AF90 clearance to proceed to the take-off runway, the 6,870 feet-long Runway 36. Wheaton and Pettit gazed at the packed slush ahead and decided the sooner they got off the ground the better. Wheaton would lift the nose wheel a little earlier than usual.

The plane rose into the air at 3.59 pm and it took the two men a matter of seconds to realise something was terribly wrong. The black box flight recorder revealed the horror of the moment.

Pettit: 'God, look at that thing . . . that doesn't seem right.'

Wheaton: 'Easy, vee-two, forward, forward. Come on, forward, forward, just barely climb.'

From behind one of the stewards yelled: 'Falling, we're falling.'

Pettit: 'Larry, we're going down Larry.'

Wheaton: 'I know it.'

Below them motorists crawling along the 14th Street Bridge heard the thundering engines before they saw the plane. Then it appeared, flying crazily low like some drunken monster reeling in the blizzard. It just managed to clear a rail bridge but then a wheel clipped the southbound highway and it dived into the frozen waters of the Potomac. Several cars were swept in with it. Eyewitnesses later gave heart-rending accounts of the 737's last moments.

Justice Department clerk Lloyd Creger said: 'The engines were so loud, they had to be going at full blast. I couldn't hear myself scream. Then I saw the plane coming out of the sky. It was just falling, but there didn't seem anything wrong with it. The nose was up and the tail was down. Then there seemed to be no sound at all.'

Local reporter Al Rossiter noted: 'There was twisted metal from crushed cars everywhere. Some of the vehicles started burning and the truck that had been hit was hanging over the edge at a 45 degree angle.'

Those who raced to the riverside from their cars were confronted by a nightmarish scene. The aircraft's fuselage had belly flopped, but because it had also snapped into three pieces most of it was sinking fast. Anguished passengers could be clearly seen through the windows, still strapped in their seats, as the icy, black waters of the Potomac bubbled up to claim them.

There were a few survivors. Most came from the tail section – the smokers' seats – and emerged scrambling across the ice. Others were thrown clear of the plane on impact and could be seen clinging to lumps of ice. Their chances of survival in the numbing water would drop dramatically after ten minutes. While they still had breath in their lungs, they screamed for help.

Unfortunately, help was delayed. Ambulances, police and fire engines were stuck in the same snarl-up as the rest of blizzard-weary Washington. To make matters worse, a subway train carrying 1000 commuters crashed minutes later, killing three of its passengers. To the harassed emergency services it must have seemed like the arrival of Armageddon.

As the minutes ticked by, a dozen police and military helicopters arrived over the river dangling ropes down to survivors. With them came choppers from the TV companies and America watched with grim fascination as the kind of disaster scenario beloved by Hollywood unfolded in real life, live, before their eyes. It was perhaps the most harrowing domestic TV footage ever broadcast.

Dozens of those in the water were already too

weak or too cold to get a firm grip on the ropes. The plight of 23-year-old stewardess Kelly Duncan was typical. She tried again and again to grasp the plastic rings hovering tantalisingly in front of her. Each time she failed.

Seconds later, helicopter pilot Donald Usher and his crewman Gene Windsor decided to risk their necks to save hers. They took the chopper down until it was almost touching the water. Then Windsor crawled out along the landing skids and hauled her aboard. She had a broken leg and severe hypothermia but she survived – the only one of the five crew to make it out alive.

Usher later denied he was a hero. Rather, he praised one unknown passenger who five times caught the rescue ring and then unselfishly passed it on to others.

'We threw the ring to him but he passed it to a man who was bleeding badly from a head injury,' said Usher. 'We went back four times, and each time he kept passing the ring to someone else, including three ladies hanging on to the tail section. The last time we went back he had gone. The ice had formed over where he had been. We stayed there ten minutes, just in hopes he had crawled into the fuselage and found an air pocket, but it became obvious he had gone.

'He's the real hero of this whole thing. If you were in his situation, 100 yards from shore and knowing that every minute you were closer to freezing to death, could you do it? I really don't think I could.'

Crewman Windsor added: 'The guy was amazing. I've never seen such guts. It seemed to me he decided that the women and the injured man needed to get out of there before him, and even as he was going under he stuck to that decision. Afterwards we looked everywhere for him but he was gone.'

The unknown hero was not the only passenger who faced death slowly. One old man found himself trapped underneath the ice, like many of the victims. Salvation Army major Harold Anderson recalled: 'He was alive when police saw him under the ice and he watched rescuers trying to get to him to get him out of the water. He was trying frantically to get out, but by the time they got the ice broken he was gone. They couldn't revive him.'

Within four hours the list of dead and injured was complete. There were only five survivors from the plane. Seven people had died on the bridge. Throughout the night the emergency services continued their harrowing task of recovering bodies from the river. Among them were a woman and her baby, floating together among the ice floes.

After seven days divers recovered the flight

recorder, the so-called 'black box', and a Federal Aviation Authority inquiry began. With so many dead, evidence from the few who made it to safety was vital. Several passengers told how they suspected a problem only seconds into the flight.

Burt Hamilton, 40, said: 'I knew something was wrong as it took off. The plane seemed to take an awful long time to pick up speed. It really started vibrating – a strong shaking, so bad that I tightened my seat belt and started to pray.'

Business executive Joe Stiley, himself a private pilot, agreed. 'Things were not going right soon after we started down the runway. We didn't have the speed. It seemed like the pilot was trying to abort, but ran out of runway. He had to make the decision to go, so we took off. We got up a little bit but it didn't climb like a normal 737. We got a fairly decent angle, then stalled and we went down. We were in the air only 20 or 30 seconds before impact.'

The crash investigators swiftly narrowed down the cause of the disaster to three possibilities – pilot error, fuel contamination, or ice on the wings. Of the three, ice emerged as the main suspect.

Less than a week before the Air Florida crash Britain's Civil Aviation Authority had contacted the FAA to report that the normally safe and reliable 737s handled badly in freezing weather.

Pilots were complaining of pitching and rolling when the wings iced up. It didn't take much ice to severely affect control.

Boeing immediately advised all airlines to check thoroughly for icing before take-off. The CAA went further, instructing pilots to increase their take-off speeds by anything up to five knots. It is some small comfort to the families of the dead that the lessons of Flight AF90 seem to have been learned.

Australian Bushfires

It was one of those Australian summers which made everyone want to decamp permanently to the swimming pool. Month after sweltering month the sun had glared down on cracked lawns and dried up river beds. Air conditioners expired, beer sales soared and cars jammed every road to the beach. By February 1983 people were praying for the luxury of a few spots of rain.

In parts of the Outback, there hadn't been so much as a shower in three years. Although unusual, this had little effect on day to day life. There were precious few settlements in the vast wilderness and the handful of roaming aborigines simply adopted the survival techniques which had served them so well over thousands of years.

In the bush it was different. Here small townships sandwiched between the major cities of the coast and the Outback eked out a living on the scrub and grassland that made up their farms. These people had known parched summers before, but nothing quite like this. They knew only too well the awesome destructive force of a bushfire and they stayed on their guard.

To help protect the homesteads, states slapped punitive fines – sometimes even jail terms – on anyone caught throwing a match or cigarette end

Australia, 1983. A primary school destroyed by bushfire sweeping across the state of Victoria.

The blaze consumed everything in its path. This entire road was engulfed before residents could even move their cars.

down carelessly. Even an empty bottle could magnify the sun's rays enough to produce the first deadly flames. Schoolchildren were taught basic fire-fighting techniques and, through the Bush Brigade and similar groups, were issued with portable water bags and hand pumps to attack any blaze they encountered. It was part of the way of life. Soon, however, it would become a way of death.

The first reports of a fire dropped at around 3.30 pm on 16 February 1983, the day known as Ash Wednesday in the Christian Church. It was centred on the Dandenong Hills, where temperature gauges had just hit 110°F in the shade, the hottest February day on record. Almost simultaneously three other major fires erupted in Victoria and a further three in South Australia, near Adelaide. It seemed the repeated warnings of state emergency services were about to come true. Much of southern Australia was a tinderbox waiting to spark.

The situation was out of control in minutes. Fanned by strong winds, bushfires are capable of advancing at 70 mph. Often they hurl huge fireballs made up of blazing oil-rich eucalyptus foliage ahead of them. In these circumstances, not even an eight-lane highway can act as an effective fire break.

The first township to be destroyed was

Cockatoo, east of Melbourne. One resident recounted how he saw the advancing flames from his verandah and made the heartbreaking decision to immediately abandon his home. It was a wise move. The fire took a mere five minutes to cover 500 yards and the timber house exploded into an inferno.

Cockatoo was a town with only one road. Some inhabitants tried to flee down it, only for the merciless flames to catch and engulf their cars. Others stayed put, hiding in cellars or makeshift underground shelters. One family survived by jumping into their water tank where, for ten hours, they feared they would be literally boiled like lobsters.

In the local school, teachers ordered 120 children to lie underneath wet blankets while their parents sprayed hoses on the roof. As one of the few brick-built buildings in Cockatoo, it was a comparatively safe place to ride out the danger.

By now armies of fire-fighters and helicopters had come to the town's rescue and were having some success in beating back the flames. Sadly, for 29 residents, it was already too late.

Elsewhere the fires raged unchecked across 100-mile fronts. Near Mount Gambier a family of five were burnt alive in their car as they accelerated through the heart of the inferno. The holiday resort of Aireys Inlet was razed to the ground, its disbelieving holidaymakers huddled together on the beach. Above them they witnessed the surrealistic sight of kangaroos leaping from the cliffs and into the waves. The terrified animals had cheated the flames, only to die drowning.

Inexorably, the burning wall began to encircle Melbourne. Its people could see the pall of smoke hanging above hills twenty miles away. They could smell death on the wind. Quietly they prayed that huge trenches which the authorities planned to dig around the city would be enough to halt the fire in its tracks.

As the disaster progressed there was occasionally morale-boosting news. At Warburton, where an entire forest was ablaze, a 700-strong team of fire-fighters and volunteers held their ground through Thursday and Friday to bring the flames under control. Though the danger of new outbreaks was described as 'perilously high' by the Victoria County Fire Service, the situation was coming under control.

Then, of course, the recriminations began. At least 71 people had died in what was now Australia's worst bushfire on record. In addition, 8,500 had lost their homes, 200,000 sheep and cattle had been roasted alive and 150,000 acres of prime farmland and forestry cultivation looked like something from a nuclear holocaust.

The public wanted to know how it could happen in a modern, technologically-advanced country.

Prime Minister Malcolm Fraser wanted to know too. He postponed his general election campaign and took on a high-profile role in handling the aftermath of the firestorm. Bankrupt farmers and growers were promised special aid, a new housing programme was launched and there were job packages for towns facing economic ruin. In the meantime, Fraser declared a weekend of national mourning.

As the soul-searching continued, it soon became obvious that there would be no easy scapegoat. No fire service in the world could have taken on that deadly wall of flame and beaten it quicker than the people of Victoria and South Australia. As to the cause of the inferno, that was a matter for argument. Some blamed arsonists, others pointed to electricity cables snapping and sparking in strong 50 mph winds. And, of course, there was that remorseless heatwave.

Perhaps there is a humbling truth behind the disaster. For all the technological achievements of mankind, there are occasions when the brute forces of nature remind us of our mortality. Whatever else could, or should, have been done to counter the fires that grim Ash Wednesday, it is unlikely to have made much difference.

Chernobyl

In early April 1986 a team of Russian physicists arrived at the Chernobyl nuclear power plant to begin a series of tests on an ageing reactor. The work was routine but the men were well aware of the awesome forces they were dealing with. Complacency should have been a dirty word.

At first all went well. The reactor worked by using uranium fuel rods to boil water, and the steam produced was then forced through turbines to produce electricity. Provided there was always enough cold water entering the system a perfect balance would be maintained. The rods would be kept cool and a steady output of steam would be emitted. As the scientists shut down the reactor to begin their tests, this stability was uppermost in their minds.

Tragically their painstaking calculations proved pointless. All it took to trigger the world's worst nuclear accident was for two men to fall asleep when they should have been on duty.

No one noticed until it was too late that the plant's water circulation system had failed. With no coolant, the uranium rods began to burn themselves – the so called 'meltdown scenario' – and temperatures at their core touched a

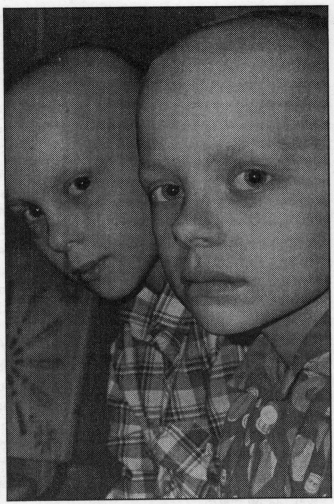

The legacy of Chernobyl: Russian children at the
Cancer Hospital in Minsk pay the price for lax safety
standards, following the nuclear power plant disaster
in 1986.

staggering 5000°F. The steam they produced was now radioactive. It reacted with a zirconium alloy casing to give off highly explosive hydrogen gas. In effect, Chernobyl had transformed itself into a nuclear bomb.

And what a bomb. The explosion produced ten times as much radiation as the US atomic devices dropped on Hiroshima and Nagasaki. Conservative estimates put the number of new Chernobyl-linked cancer cases at 150,000 within 10 years. A poison cloud of radioactivity swept east across Europe as far as the hill farms of Wales and Cumbria in the UK and down the west coast of France. Hundreds of thousands of beef cattle and lambs were declared unfit for consumption. And what was Moscow's reaction? The communist rulers kept quiet.

Yet such was the enormity of the Chernobyl disaster that this was one news item even the Kremlin could not control for long. At 9 am on 28 April Swedish technicians at Forsmark nuclear power station, 60 miles outside Stockholm, began picking up bizarre Geiger-count readings on their computer screens. Persistent warning bleeps told them that a massive radiation leak was taking place.

Desperately, the team began checking all monitoring equipment and gauges to try and pin it down. It was a fruitless exercise. Forsmark was operating normally yet every one of its 600 workers had been exposed to levels at least four times above approved safety limits. The Swedish scientists called Stockholm and broke the bad news. The Soviet Union seemed to be the source.

It was not until 9 pm that night that Moscow finally owned up. A brief item on the evening news reported a statement from the authorities which read:

'An accident has taken place at the at the Chernobyl power station and one of the reactors was damaged. Measures are being taken to eliminate the consequences of the accident. Those affected by it are being given assistance. A government commission has been set up.' Scarcely pausing for breath, the newscaster moved on to his next story about a new Soviet peace fund.

It was a scandalous way to report the worst accident in 32 years of commercial nuclear power. And it revealed nothing of the heroic fire-fighters who, at that very moment, were killing themselves from exposure to radiation.

The officer leading the fire teams, Lieutenant-Colonel Leonid Telyatnikov, had been called to the scene at 1.32 am on 26 April, exactly nine minutes after the explosion. Later he described his first sight of the crippled reactor.

'I had no idea what had happened or what we

were heading into,' he recounted. 'But as I approached the plant I could see debris on fire all around like sparklers. Then I noticed a bluish glow above the wreckage of reactor four and pockets of fire on surrounding buildings. It was absolutely silent.'

Telyatnikov and his 28 men began fighting the flames protected by nothing more than a hard hat and wellington boots. The Chernobyl reactor had begun pumping more than 100,000,000 curies of radiation into the atmosphere and within minutes the first fire-fighters had sustained lethal doses. Telyatnikov recalled:

'I realised it was not an ordinary situation as soon as I passed through the gate. There was just the noise of machines and the fire crackling. The fire-fighters knew what they had to do and proceeded quietly, on the run. The radiation-measuring meters had frozen on their highest level. Thoughts of my family would flash through my mind and be gone. No one would discuss the radiation risk. The most frightening thought was that we wouldn't have enough strength to hold out until reserves came.

'About an hour after the blaze began a group of fire-fighters with symptoms of radiation exposure were taken down from a rooftop close to the damaged reactor. When I approached five men to take up the position they rushed to the building's rooftop almost before I could get the words out of my mouth. They are all dead now from radiation poisoning.'

Neither did Telyatnikov escape the dreadful effects of the fire. For years after he was one of the Chernobyl veterans dubbed 'the living dead' by Russians and his life became a constant battle against cancer.

Three days into the disaster and still the Soviet hierarchy was playing it down. Moscow at first rejected offers of scientific help from Stockholm, regarding that as unnecessary Western meddling. However as the extent of the crisis became apparent they asked West German experts for advice on extinguishing graphite core reactor fires. A US expert in bone marrow transplants, Dr Robert Gale, was asked to help treat the worst-affected radiation victims.

Slowly the Kremlin began to recognise that international uproar was inevitable. An up-and-coming Soviet politician called Boris Yeltsin gave the first public hint of what was to come:

'It is serious, very serious,' he said. 'The cause apparently lies in human error. We are undertaking measures to make sure this doesn't happen again.'

It took a week to put the fire out and by then hundreds of soldiers and fire-fighters had received potentially lethal doses of radiation. Helicopters dropped tonnes of wet sand and lead on top of the burning reactor in an attempt to smother the flames. Boron, an element which soaks up radioactive neutrons, was also scattered around.

Yet throughout the damage-limitation operation the Soviets seemed to have no clear planning strategy. Devoid of any better idea, they resorted to digging an enormous pit into which they bulldozed contaminated soil, bits of burnt out reactor and the clothes of the disaster team. This deadly cocktail of debris was then covered with 2,000,000 cubic feet of concrete.

As snippets of intelligence information on the disaster trickled out, Western governments began to grow impatient. Nuclear experts were aghast at the shoddy way in which the Soviets had taken safety precautions. Had the doomed reactor been covered with a concrete outer shell – standard design in the West – much of the fire and radiation could have been contained.

In an address to the American nation, President Ronald Reagan insisted:

'The Soviets owe the world an explanation. A full accounting of what happened at Chernobyl and what is happening now is the least the world community has a right to expect.'

Meanwhile the daunting task of evacuating 100,000 people living within an 18-mile radius of the plant continued. Within a few months the first legacies of Chernobyl were emerging; mutated calves and lambs, stillborn babies, blood disorders and deformed vegetation. Later, statisticians would discover the number of leukaemia cases in Minsk alone had doubled.

Ignoring world criticism, Moscow found suitable scapegoats in the two Chernobyl workers who had fallen asleep – director Viktor Bryukhanov and chief engineer Anatoly Dyatlov. Both men were jailed for dereliction of duty.

The official estimate of casualties was a farce. It claimed there were 31 dead, 1000 injured and the likelihood of 6000 directly-attributable cancer deaths over the next 70 years. Shortly before the break-up of the Soviet Union, ex-President Gorbachev admitted the figures had been massaged. Senior officials at the Kremlin actually believed Western radiation experts were closer to the truth. The death toll could yet be 250,000.

Zeebrugge

It should have been just another hop across the English Channel for the car ferry *Herald of Free Enterprise*. Most of her 436 passengers were seasoned seafarers and regarded the 4-hour voyage from Zeebrugge to Dover as no more risky than catching a bus to work. Their minds were on trivialities. Had they bought enough duty-frees? Should they have a full fried supper? How long would the drive home take?

Many were travelling on a special one-day return ticket provided by one of Britain's daily newspapers. As they settled into seats in the bars and restaurants, just about the last thing on their minds was the ship's safety. Weather forecasts for the evening of 6 March 1987 predicted slightly choppy seas, typical for the time of year.

At 6.05 pm, Captain David Lewry eased his 7,951-tonne vessel away from pier number 12 and headed west. One of Townsend Thoresen's longest-serving skippers, he had completed the voyage many times and knew the procedures off by heart. Among the strict rules to observe before sailing was the closing of the bow doors, through which the *Herald* had admitted her cargo of 40 lorries and 80 cars.

Captain Lewry assumed this had been done as

Zeebrugge, 1987. A tugboat struggles to keep afloat the listing *Herald of Free Enterprise* in which 193 passengers drowned.

he cast off the moorings. He could not see the bows from the bridge but he knew that a crew member would have been assigned responsibility for operating the doors. As a safety precaution, the Chief Officer was also expected to double-check that they were shut.

Many masters were not happy with this system. For a start, they knew that the design of their ships was inherently unseaworthy. Ocean-going vessels are normally equipped with water-tight bulkheads to seal off sections inside the hull. If there is a leak, flooding can often be confined to the area of damage.

Car ferries, on the other hand, rely on vast open areas for quick and efficient parking. If water pours in, it is free to slosh around the vehicle decks instantly destabilising the ship.

The fact that Townsend Thoresen captains recognised this danger is obvious from a memo one of them sent to the crew of the *Herald*'s sister ship, the *Pride of Free Enterprise*, three years earlier. It read:

'Twice since going on the Zeebrugge run, this ship has sailed with the stern or bow doors open. No doubt this is caused by job/rank changes from the Calais run; however, all those named persons must see that the system is worked to make sure this dangerous situation does not occur. Give it your utmost attention.'

In June 1985 another of the *Pride*'s skippers asked the fleet's managing director to install 'doors closed' indicators on the bridges of all vessels. This, he argued, would enable all captains to be absolutely certain they were putting to sea safely. The reply he got from one shore-based official was scathing: 'Do they need an indicator to tell them whether the deck storekeeper is awake and sober? My goodness.' The author would live to regret his words.

The seaman in charge of the doors as the *Herald* left Zeebrugge was Assistant Boatswain Mark Stanley. He was asleep in his bunk. The officer charged with ensuring he performed his duty was Chief Officer Leslie Sable. Sable didn't check up.

As a result the doors stayed open. Twenty minutes into the voyage, just as the *Herald* left the shelter of Zeebrugge's three-mile-long sea wall defence the waves became large enough to lap over the open doors and into her hull. A night of terror had begun.

There was panic on the main passenger decks as the ferry suddenly listed, partially righted herself and then toppled onto her side like some mortally-wounded sea monster. She lay in barely 30 feet of water, the whole of her starboard clearly visible. In the first 45 seconds of the disaster her hull had half-filled with water.

Dozens of people died in those first chaotic minutes, sucked down in the torrents that raged through the ship. Other passengers drowned in the rest rooms or their private cabins. Screaming survivors flailed about in the blackness, unable to orientate themselves in the surreal environment which surrounded them. Stairs ran sideways while passageways turned into sheer pits dropping into an unforgiving, freezing sea.

One eye witness, Irish lorry driver Larry O'Brian, recalled how the only warning of impending disaster was when plates flew off the tables in the ship's restaurant.

'People were sucked out through portholes like you see in those movies about air disasters,' he said. 'They didn't have a chance. And the boat – well, when I was being taken off it and I looked back at it, it looked like something out of the Second World War that was hit with torpedoes.'

One of the passengers on the newspaper special-offer ticket was 30-year-old Andrew Simmons from Bushey, near London.

He recalled: 'We were trapped for 20 or 30 minutes after the boat went over. Within a minute it went from being upright to on its side with water gushing in down the stairs and corridors. I and my friend helped a little girl, who was only two or three years old, climb up with her father above the water. We were only rescued when

Hundreds of unused life jackets sum up the awful scale of the catastrophe.

The battered remains of the vehicles that were inside the ferry when disaster struck.

people smashed the windows from outside and hauled us out to safety.'

In those desperate hours, heroes would emerge performing the most unlikely deeds. Londoner Andrew Parker formed himself into a human bridge by stretching his body across the rising waters. Around 120 people crawled to safety over him and his bravery was later recognised with the George Medal.

Then there was the Belgian naval frogman, Lieutenant Guido Couwenbergh, who was one of the first rescue workers to arrive. With little thought for his own safety he managed to pull 40 people out of the wreck, all of them numb with shock and cold. Couwenbergh later received the Queen's Medal for Gallantry.

One survivor, teenager Nicola Simpson from Hertfordshire, had a body temperature 25 degrees below normal; a state of hypothermia which meant she was clinically dead. Amazingly, she was resuscitated and made a full recovery. She owes her life to Belgian civilian diver, Piet Lagast, who smashed a thick sheet of glass to reach her, almost chopping off his hand in the process. He too was given the QMG.

As the minutes ticked by, more and more rescue craft began to move in. The British warships *HMS Glasgow* and *HMS Diomede* helped coordinate naval helicopters from

Culdrose in combing waters around the wreck for signs of survivors. One chopper pilot said later: 'I could see black shapes bobbing in the water, arms splayed out like jellyfish. I knew they were dead.'

Meanwhile hospitals in Zeebrugge were put on red alert to tackle the major disaster. Off-duty doctors and nurses were rounded up and requests for assistance were passed to other hospitals along the coast. Predictably, there were not enough beds to go around.

Back in England, news of the disaster had filtered onto the 9 pm news. Worried relatives began assembling at Dover docks to demand more information and found hordes of TV, radio and newspaper reporters already there waiting. In the fear and frustration of the moment, some of the journalists were attacked.

Within 48 hours the scale of the disaster had struck home. Almost 4 in every 10 passengers died, a total of 193 victims, and survivors needed hospital treatment. For dozens of survivors the legacy of Zeebrugge would be a ceaselessly repeated nightmare. Years later, many continued to seek treatment for post-traumatic stress.

In July 1987 a 29-day inquiry conducted by Mr Justice Sheen concluded the ship sunk because neither Mr Stanley nor Mr Sable did their jobs properly. Senior master John Kirby was also criticised for his conduct. Ultimate responsibility, said the judge, rested with Captain Lewry. It was, after all, his ship.

But the criticism didn't end there. Justice Sheen was determined that Townsend Thoresen should not escape condemnation for the 'disease of sloppiness' which seemed to affect the entire company. Shore-based officials, he said, were guilty of 'staggering complacency' in failing to respond to the concerns of their masters.

The judge went on: 'By the autumn of 1986 the shore staff of the company were well aware of the possibility that one of their ships would sail with her stern or bow doors open. This topic has been discussed at length because it shows the attitude of the marine department (of T.T.) to suggestions made by the masters.'

Later an inquest jury at Dover decided that all the dead passengers had been unlawfully killed. A prosecution was mounted against Captain Lewry and some of the other officers, but this was later dropped. It was evident to everyone that the men would suffer for the rest of their lives.

The *Herald* was eventually righted by giant floating cranes and, in what was to be her last voyage, towed to Taiwan. There, bolt by bolt, she was broken up in a dockside scrapyard, an ignoble end for an infamous ship.

Soccer

For more than 100 years, soccer has been Britain's best-loved sport. Even the combination of falling crowds, drunken hooligans and expensive seats have failed to quell the ardour of hundreds of thousands of fans who religiously follow their team's fortunes.

One of the greatest managers the game has ever seen, Liverpool's Bill Shankly, summed up the British love affair with its national sport in an oft-repeated quote. 'Football,' he quipped, 'isn't a matter of life and death. It's much more important than that.'

Tragically, three horrendous stadium disasters in the mid to late eighties showed in graphic terms that he was wrong. Watching football had become, quite literally, a matter of life and death.

Up until 1985, the thought that a catastrophe could strike at a league football match had never even occurred to most fans. True, a few veterans of the terraces remembered the Ibrox Stadium disaster of 1971 when, in the dying seconds of the game, Glasgow Rangers scored an equaliser against their deadliest rivals, Glasgow Celtic. Rangers fans who had been pouring out of the ground, resigned to defeat, heard the roar and turned to run back inside. Chaos and panic

Bradford, 1985. Fans take refuge on the pitch as the wooden stand goes up in flames.

Nothing can be done as the 'tinder box' stand burns, leaving 56 people dead.

One family lost members of three generations to the inferno that gutted this stand.

ensued, safety barriers collapsed and 66 people were suffocated to death.

But fourteen years later, as home supporters flocked to Bradford's stadium eager to watch the local promotion contenders, crowd safety was not much of a talking point on the terraces. Fans were in the mood for an early celebration and the gate was higher than usual.

The ground had seen better days. Much of it was built of wood and beneath the seats of the main touchline stand years of discarded rubbish lay in huge heaps. It was out of sight, out of mind as far as club officials were concerned.

Later, pre-decimal coins were found by rescue workers sifting through the smoke-blackened wreckage of the stand. It was perhaps fifteen or twenty years since this hidden part of the ground had seen a broom.

Close to half time a fan – we shall never know who – dropped either a cigarette end or a match through the floorboards beneath his seat and onto the tinderbox of fuel below. Soon fire started to smoulder, spreading rapidly. Then, suddenly, a large area of rubbish exploded into flames and dozens of seats were alight. The flames licked upwards, setting fire to the roof, before spreading out along the whole length of the stand.

For those inside it was a horrifying scenario.

There were no fire extinguishers – they had been taken away to prevent hooligans using them as weapons. There were no emergency exits – the doors at the rear of the stand had been bolted to thwart gatecrashers. Screaming fans were burnt alive, many from the flaming tarpaulin fabric which dropped from the blazing roof and smothered them in a blanket of fire.

Fifty-six people died, including two children. In one case three generations of a family were instantly wiped out; an eleven year old, his father and grandfather. The only survivors were those who managed to scramble onto the pitch.

Two weeks later, while British football was still mourning the Bradford fire victims, tragedy struck again. The setting was the Heysel football stadium in Brussels where Liverpool Football Club, then one of the world's greatest teams, were due to play Italian league giants Juventus.

From the start this European Cup final – still the most prestigious club match in the world – seemed dogged with controversy and ill-will. There was obvious tension on the streets beforehand, with the supporters of both sides involved in taunting and running brawls. When the ground opened, and police penned a block of Italian fans at the end of the ground reserved for Liverpool, it seemed to be asking for trouble. Before a ball had been kicked, trouble arrived.

Some Liverpool supporters broke out of their own enclosure and raced across a neutral zone hurling bricks and lumps of metal at the Juventus followers. The Italians tried to escape the onslaught by cramming themselves at the bottom of the stand against a concrete wall. Part of this was already unsafe and now it collapsed. A sea of humanity toppled over it and onto the pitch.

Anyone who witnessed those scenes of panic and death will remember it for the rest of their lives. Incompetent police officers swinging batons as people suffocated, fighting between rival fans on the pitch and through the mayhem the screams of the dying. It took three-quarters of an hour for the first medical help to arrive and by the time order was restored the death toll was 39, 33 of whom were Italian. One Briton died, a man who just happened to be in Brussels and thought he'd attend his first football match.

European soccer's governing body, UEFA, later temporarily banned English clubs from European cup competitions.

The final horror in what had become a decade of soccer stadium disasters also proved the most costly in terms of human life. This time, it was Liverpool's turn to taste the tears of tragedy.

On 15 April 1989 fans from Liverpool and Nottingham Forest descended on the Yorkshire steel town of Sheffield to watch an FA Cup semi-

Heysel, 1985. Belgian riot police move in at the
European Cup Final between Liverpool and Juventus.

All that remains of the wall which collapsed when
Juventus fans tried to escape from Liverpool fans – 39
people were crushed to death.

final game. Sheffield Wednesday's cavernous Hillsborough stadium had been chosen to host the match for two reasons. First it was neutral ground. Second it was thought to be big enough to accommodate the huge travelling support anticipated by both sides. A capacity gate of 54,000 was a certainty.

Sheffield police had not had long to plan the management of this large crowd but they had plenty of experience in policing league football. Sheffield had two prestigious league clubs – Wednesday and United – and officers knew the importance of segregating rival fans before and after a game. It was established policy to delay a kick-off only as a last resort. Delay only caused further disruption to the city's residents.

The turnstiles opened soon after midday but it became noticeable that the West Stand, allocated to Liverpool supporters, was slow in filling up. Officers searching for alcohol and offensive weapons at the Leppings Lane entrance found they had plenty of time to question fans. There were no large queues.

By 2 pm, some senior officers were privately wondering what had happened to Liverpool's support. Experience suggested there should have been around 20,000 Liverpool supporters in place, whereas in fact there was little more than half that number. In the West Stand only enclosures 3 and 4, which boasted the best views of the goal, were filling up. Nottingham Forest's end of the ground was populated as expected.

It occurred to police that thousands of Liverpool fans would be arriving late and determined not to miss a second of their most important match so far in the 1988/89 season. Yet Superintendent Duckenfield, the senior officer in charge, ruled that it was not necessary to delay kick off. He clung to the belief that the fans would still get in by 3 pm.

In fact the sheer weight of cars and coaches making the trek across the Pennines from Merseyside made Duckenfield's assessment optimistic in the extreme. As the minutes ticked by to kick-off, queues outside the Lepping Lane turnstiles grew exponentially, to the point that many hundreds were arriving while only a handful per minute were being admitted.

By 2.45 pm the situation was fast becoming untenable. Seeing the crush in front of them, previously good-humoured fans began to get frustrated. Others deliberately tried to push their way to the front, oblivious to the effects their actions would have on others.

That said, the police handling of the crisis left much to be desired. Inside the ground hundreds of supporters continued to try and pack their way into the popular 3 and 4 pens. The resulting logjam meant fans queuing behind could not get into the other enclosures. Outside there were 5000 fans angrily demanding the chance to get in.

The senior officer in charge at the Leppings Lane end radioed Duckenfield recommending that exit barriers be swung open to let the fans in en masse. But the Superintendent could not make an immediate decision. It was not until eight minutes before kick-off that he agreed to open the gates. Within minutes, 2000 fans were clawing their way through, with or without tickets. The vast majority made straight for the areas deemed to give the best view – pens 3 and 4. They could not know, because they could not see, that down at the front the first victims were already choking and suffocating to death.

The crush on these fans intensified as the teams took the field. Those still conscious screamed and begged police on touchline duty to open emergency exits in the wire security fencing around the pitch. Their pleas went unheeded. Officers thought they were either cheering on their team or trying to wave to the BBC TV cameras which were broadcasting the match live.

One group of supporters managed to open the gate to pen 3. Police, trained to spot a pitch invasion in the offing, immediately rallied round and closed it. Other Liverpool fans caught climbing the wire were pushed back like prisoners of war being subjugated by their camp guards. Some were jammed and immobilised against crush barriers or fencing. Others began to slip beneath the sea of bodies. And all the time the steady shove from behind them continued.

Four minutes into the match, Liverpool England star Peter Beardsley struck a sweetly-timed shot which cannoned off the Forest crossbar. In the West Stand excited fans lunged forward and the surge snapped a crush barrier which was already fatally weakened. Dozens of fans disappeared from view. Many had gasped their last breath or, deprived of oxygen for four minutes, suffered irreparable brain damage.

At last the police, for so long on their guard against a pitch invasion, saw the hideous truth. The senior officer at Liverpool's end of the ground radioed Duckenfield warning that the match would have to be stopped. He didn't bother to hear the reply. Instead he raced out among the players, grabbed the referee and urged him to lead both teams off. It was five minutes past three. In the West Stand, 95 fans were either dead or dying.

The security fence access to pens 3 and 4 was now flung open and police began the grotesque task of trying to disentangle the barely alive from the bodies of the dead. Young PCs stared in disbelief at a sight that would traumatise them for years to come: faces coloured deep blue from oxygen deprivation; corpses with eyes open, tongues lolling; unseeing eyes staring; the smell of vomit and faeces infused the air. Policemen who had buttoned up their uniform that morning in preparation to confront soccer thugs suddenly found themselves taking on the duties of front-line medics. In shock and anger some surviving fans began kicking and spitting at the officers, which served only to heighten the confusion.

Most of Hillsborough's dead were young men in their twenties. Only 7 were women and only 3 of the 95 were aged 50 or more. They all had one thing in common – death from asphyxiation.

Nowhere was the tragedy felt deeper than at Anfield, Liverpool's home ground. Within minutes of the first news reports, Merseysiders began arriving with makeshift bouquets of flowers in memory of the dead. At first these were dropped outside the entrance gates. But as the scale of the tragedy became clear, club officials ordered the turnstiles to be opened. Within hours the goal in front of the famous Kop terrace was covered in blooms, scarves and messages of sympathy. Some fans linked arms and, through their sobs, sung the Liverpool anthem *You'll Never Walk Alone.*

Earthquake!

Housewife Annette Henry described being in a city struck by an earthquake in these emotively descriptive words: 'It was as if God had just clapped his hands. The ground was like a wave underneath a surfboard, and the cars on the highway were jumping up and down like in a Walt Disney movie. Every time we have an earthquake in California we giggle, we're cool, we're blasé about it. This time was different. I was just hanging on, thinking, 'It's not so funny any more.' I thought we were having the Big One.'

The earth tremor that Annette Henry was talking about was the Great San Francisco Earthquake of October 1989. In fact, the quake started twelve miles beneath the craggy hills of Los Gatos, 75 miles south-east of San Francisco, and shook its way through the ground until it hit the city during the evening rush hour on Tuesday 17 October.

Within fifteen seconds the quake had reduced many buildings to rubble, had started fires through the historic Marina district, had ruptured thousands of miles of gas and water mains, had destroyed a section of the famous Oakland Bay Bridge and had collapsed a mile-long section of elevated highway.

It was this collapse of Interstate 880 that was responsible for most of the 100 deaths in the city that day, as the upper deck of the bridge concertinaed onto the lower roadway, trapping cars and crushing their occupants under thousands of tons of reinforced concrete.

Another drama occurred on the double-decked Oakland Bay Bridge, when a span of the upper roadway crashed onto the lower deck, leaving an impassable 50 feet gap. A woman driver gunned her car in a vain attempt to leap the chasm. Instead, she fell into the void.

As fires burned through the night, however, the city of San Francisco, lying across the geologically volatile San Andreas Fault, counted itself lucky to have survived with so few injuries and fatalities. For the 1989 quake had not been the 'Big One'. It had only one-fortieth of the power of an earlier earthquake which literally shook the city to its early foundations.

The infamous 1906 San Francisco Earthquake struck shortly after five in the afternoon on Wednesday 18 April and reached an astonishing 8.3 on the Richter Scale.

The entire city shook. Tall buildings swayed, shook and crumbled. The very earth rose and fell as if tossed on a subterranean sea. The 'earthquake-proof' City Hall was destroyed. Mansions collapsed and the new, luxurious,

Italy, 1980. Rescue teams search for survivors in the debris caused by six earthquakes in the area between Naples and Salerno – 2614 people were killed.

$7,000,000 *Palace Hotel* was reduced to rubble. (One of the guests, singer Enrico Caruso, left not his heart but his stomach in San Francisco and vowed never to return.)

The population of the city was then only 340,000 – but 250,0000 of them were left homeless. The earthquake left relatively few dead only because there had been earlier warning shocks in 1898 and 1900. But the death toll was bad enough: 800 people perished in collapsing buildings and in the firestorms that swept through the streets in the quake's wake. For the geological damage did not compare with that caused by the ensuing fires – which burned eight square miles comprising several hundred blocks.

Writer Jack London mourned: 'San Francisco is gone! Nothing remains of it but memories and a fringe of dwelling houses on the outskirts. All the cunning adjustments of a twentieth century city have been smashed by the earthquake. The streets have been humped into ridges and piled with the debris of fallen walls. All the shrewd contrivances and safeguards of man have been thrown out of gear by 30 seconds' twitching of the earth's crust!'

The author could have been speaking in about almost any of the major earthquakes that have shaken the planet's flimsy fabric since people began building cities for nature to knock down.

The most disastrous losses from a single earthquake were recorded in the Shensi province of China on 23 January 1556, when no fewer than 830,000 people perished in two hours of shock-waves. About 300,000 people are believed to have lost their lives in a Calcutta earthquake in 1737. And even in Britain, never noted as an earthquake area, more than 1000 buildings were damaged and 5 people died in Colchester, Essex, when the worst quake ever to hit the country struck in 1884.

Japan is one of the seismic 'capitals' of the globe. A major earthquake struck that country in 1923 when a news flash from Tokyo on 2 September read: 'Yokohama and most of Tokyo totally destroyed in devastating earthquake followed by fire.' As many as 100,000 died, most of them not in the quake itself but in the fire cyclone that followed the shock. A trainload of passengers suffocated in a tunnel, rivers broke their banks drowning thousands, and a tidal wave killed still more.

But the threat has not gone away. Other major earthquakes that have 'twitched the planet', as Jack London put it, during the shaky course of recent history include:

1960, Morocco. A string of shocks, culminating in one that lasted an incredible 10 seconds, reduced the town of Agadir to rubble and killed about 10,000 people on the night of 2 March. In the Atlas Mountains, the earth cracked and swallowed villagers by the dozen. A hydrographic survey later revealed that an offshore seabed that had once been charted at 1,200 feet now lay at 45 feet.

1960, Chile. On 21 May the town of Concepcion, southern Chile, was largely demolished for the fifth time in its history. Four thousand people died and resultant tidal waves caused damage ten thousand miles away in Japan.

1970, Peru. Fifty miles off the Pacific coast, the ocean bed cracked and heaved on the afternoon of 1 May, and the shock affected the mainland from Trujillo to Lima, Peru. The full death toll will never be known – but the devastation covered an area the size of Scotland and the consequent avalanches alone killed 30,000 in the Yungay mountain region.

1972, Nicaragua. An earthquake only days before Christmas virtually destroyed the Nicaraguan capital of Managua. Two jolts in the early hours of 22 December cost the lives of between 11,000 and 12,000 people. More than 30,000 (75 per cent of the city's population) were rendered homeless. All firefighting equipment was lost and it was not until daybreak that emergency services arrived from neighbouring Costa Rica.

Mexico, 1985. The devastating earthquake that hit Mexico City brought the corner of this building crashing to the ground.

1976, China. One of history's least documented earthquakes was also one of the worst. An estimated 750,000 died on 28 July in the area around the industrial city of Tangshan, in the Tientsin region. Buildings were damaged far away in Beijing.

1977, Rumania. A quake hit the 'Dracula' country – the Transylvania region, north of Bucharest – on 4 March, killing 1,400 people.

1978, Iran. Forty villages in north-east Iran were destroyed on 19 September when quakes killed more than 26,000. In one town, Tabas, only 2000 of the 13,000 population survived.

1980, Italy. Six violent earthquakes hit the area between Naples and Salerno on 26 November, resulting in 2,614 deaths. The survivors suffered severe blizzards and a second, minor earthquake a month later.

1994, Los Angeles. A shock of 6.6 on the Richter Scale killed 61 people on the night of 17 January. Fearing a second quake, panic-stricken drivers packed the freeways – only to find several of them breached by the shock-waves.

In fact, a second shock did come, but not until 20 March. At 5.3 on the Richter Scale, it was not as severe as its predecessor and caused little damage despite its 30-second duration. But it shook up the Hollywood stars who were preparing for that night's Oscar presentations!

It was also a salutary lesson to the inward-looking Californians that the power of personality is a microcosm against the awesome power of nature. Los Angeles lies along the same San Andreas Fault that moved in 1906 and destroyed an entire city – when a single earthquake 'twitched the planet'.

1995, Japan. A quake, measuring 7.2 on the Richter scale, caused thousands of buildings to collapse and started a huge fire, principally in Kobe, but also in Osaka and Kyoto. More than 3000 people were killed, another 1000 injured and 250,000 made homeless. This was seen by many as the precursor of the 'mega quake' that threatens Japan.

The Exxon Valdez

The atmosphere in the *Pipeline Club* at Valdez, Alaska, was thick with the fumes of tobacco and alcohol. It was the kind of place beloved by seamen and oilmen and on the evening of 23 March 1989, both trades were well represented. When Captain Joseph Hazelwood walked in with two of his officers to down a few beers, hardly a head turned.

Hazelwood was a familiar face at the *Pipeline*, though an irregular customer there. The 42-year-old skipper of the supertanker, *Exxon Valdez*, earned his living ferrying millions of barrels of Alaskan crude oil to the ever-thirsty refineries of California and Texas. He enjoyed a drink whenever he put into Valdez, especially if he was facing a long trip. True, the Exxon company had a strict rule banning consumption of alcohol in the four hours before a voyage. But Hazelwood liked to interpret that flexibly.

Later, he would live to regret every gulp of the four beers he put away. Within a few hours his vessel would be grounded on a razor-sharp reef in Prince William Sound, dumping 40,000 tonnes of its viscous black cargo onto one of the world's most environmentally sensitive coastlines. The accident left Hazelwood portrayed as a captain

Alaska, 1989. A smaller tanker tries to off-load crude oil from the *Exxon Valdez* which spilt over 270,000 barrels of oil.

drunk in charge of his ship. It was an unfair label but one the public easily identified with. It stuck!

Valdez was transformed into an oil boom town in the mid-seventies and quickly became one of the most important supertanker ports in the world. The city's prominence emerged almost as an afterthought – the original plan was to run a pipeline from the newly-discovered Alaskan oilfield through Canada to the Mid-West and northern California. But America's oil tycoons felt uneasy about having their precious asset pumped across a foreign country. It was decided to build a 789-mile pipeline to Valdez, and let tankers do the remaining 2000-plus miles south.

The city has done well out of the boom. A community that once lived desperately close to the poverty line has been inundated with new oil jobs, and consequently bulging wage packets. Even the pipeline itself has proved a major attraction. Tourists queue in their droves to see the 48-inch diameter steel pipe, comprising 101,850 sections, vanish into the northern wilderness.

Such is the huge Alaskan oil output that captains like Joe Hazelwood spent most of their time on the Valdez-West Coast run. The procedures for entering and exiting port were etched in Hazelwood's memory and he knew the waters of the Sound like the roads round his home on Long Island, New York. He did not regard the waters as particularly difficult to navigate. Some would later accuse him of complacency.

At 8 pm Hazelwood and his drinking companions, third mate Gregory Cousins and able seaman Robert Kagan, were back aboard the *Exxon Valdez*. At 9.10 pm the 211,469-tonne vessel slipped her moorings to begin the voyage to Long Beach, California. It was an hour earlier than her scheduled sailing time but the US Coastguard Vessel Traffic Control centre had given the all-clear. For the next two hours and twenty minutes, harbour pilot William Murphy would have control.

Shortly after Murphy had left the ship to return to port on a launch, Hazelwood made two course changes. He was concerned about ice showing on the radar and asked traffic control if he could switch to the clearer inbound sea lane. The controller gave permission, assuring him there were no inbound ships in the vicinity.

Hazelwood planned to clear the ice below Busby Island before heading south-west in a narrow passage between the underwater rocks of Bligh Reef and another major ice floe. It was a tricky manoeuvre but not one the captain pondered too long. In fact he was so confident that he planned to hand the entire operation over to Cousins as soon as possible.

Hazelwood's style of captaincy was a hands-off approach. He was a highly skilled master and believed the best way to teach his juniors the ropes was to delegate as much responsibility as possible. He certainly had few worries about 38-year-old Gregory Cousins' competency. In a staff evaluation report the previous year he had rated his third mate as having 'excellent navigational skills' though 'only average knowledge of ship handling characteristics'.

In the half-hour between 11.30 pm and midnight. Hazelwood made two of his most questionable decisions. The first was to give the order 'load program up', an instruction to activate the ship's computer program responsible for regulating build-up to full sea speed. The second was to engage the auto-pilot. With considerable ice about, many masters would have thought twice before relinquishing manual control – especially when a junior such as Cousins was watch officer.

It is possible that fondness for drink affected the captain's judgement. But, some maritime experts have argued, complacency is an equally dangerous trait. Was it possible that because Hazelwood was such a talented mariner, he could not imagine the problems less gifted men might face? From the moment Hazelwood left the bridge just before midnight, Gregory Cousins' watch proved one big problem.

He had been instructed to make a right hand turn back into the outbound sea lane after reaching a navigational point near Busby Island. But, unaccountably, Cousins waited six minutes too long before starting the turn. As a result the tanker was a mile further ahead than she should have been.

At six minutes past midnight the ship had moved to a course of 247 degrees, a major change which helmsman Robert Kagan felt should be corrected. He tried to slow the swing before Cousins ordered: 'Hard right rudder.' By now both men could clearly see they were way off line and consequently Cousins made a desperate phone call to his captain. 'I think we are in serious trouble,' he said.

Hazelwood already knew it. A few seconds earlier he had felt a terrible, juddering welling up from the bowels of the ship. He guessed they had run onto the reef and his principal fear as he sprinted to the bridge was that if part of the hull slipped she could break her back. A fully laden crude carrier the size of three football pitches would be at the mercy of the waves.

As the crisis unfolded, Hazelwood produced a text book response. By carefully varying his engine power he was able to keep the *Exxon Valdez* tight to the reef, ensuring her stability. If drink had given him a fuzzy head, the prospect of a giant oil slick now brought his thoughts sharply back into focus.

Below water the ship's hull had sustained rents up to sixteen feet long. Eight of the fifteen holds had been penetrated and crude oil was already in the sea. In the days ahead, 10,000,000 gallons would be lost.

For years the major players in the US oil market had played down the risk of environmental disaster on this scale. Only two years earlier a consortium of companies had stated confidentially: 'It is highly unlikely that there will ever be a spill of any magnitude.' Yet only two months earlier a relatively tiny spill of 1,500 barrels had pushed their fast-reaction clean-up team to its limits. In Prince William Sound that team was right out of its league.

For a start it took ten hours to get them to the scene. They arrived with no booms – vital equipment if a slick is to be contained – and their detergents proved useless because the sea was too calm. Attempts to burn off the crude oil proved a waste of time. And the US Coastguard, required by law to have a vessel on hand for damage-control operations, transparently failed in its duty. Its tiny fleet was cruising 2000 miles away off San Francisco.

By Sunday 26 March the slick covered 900 square miles. It polluted the hundreds of remote, rocky coves that run the length of Prince William Sound and once these were fouled there was little hope of keeping it together. An estimated 86,000 birds, 1,000 sea otters, 25,000 fish, 200 seals and dozens of beavers were all killed. The oil lingered in the coves, destroying thousands of young fish which return each year to spawn in the shallows.

America was in uproar at news of the incident, portrayed by the media as the worst on record. In fact, the *Exxon Valdez* slick ranks only tenth in the league of oil tanker disasters. It was but a seventh the size of the Amoco Cadiz leak which hit North-West France in March 1977. And it was only an eighth as big as the world's worst oil tanker spillage caused by the collision of the *Aegean Captain* and the *Atlantic Empress* off Tobago in the Caribbean in 1979.

Captain Hazelwood was summarily dismissed. Exxon said blood alcohol tests taken nine hours after the ship grounded proved he had been drinking in breach of company rules. In any case, he had already been tried and convicted by the media. Newspapers told how, in 1985, he went on a 28-day stint to a drying-out clinic near New York. The treatment followed his conviction for drunken driving the previous year. Hazelwood also had a reputation among *Exxon* crew for livening up long voyages with parties.

If Exxon hoped Hazelwood would prove a

handy scapegoat, it was wrong. Later inquiries concluded he acted with honour and initiative after the accident. Moreover, they expressed concern about the fatigue of his crew. *Exxon Valdez* was one of the largest vessels afloat, yet her manning had been reduced in recent years from twenty-four to twenty.

The implications for Exxon were huge. Full-page newspaper advertisements were taken out urging a consumer boycott of its products. Petrol stations across the country stood empty following accusations that the company had not responded to the leak with enough gusto. Exxon President Frank Iarossi was forced to respond by promising a hefty $1 billion to assist with the clean up exercise and compensate fishermen for their lost livelihoods.

Since the disaster, tougher rules have been imposed on seamen who drink directly before a voyage. New tankers are being designed with a double hull, an excellent safety feature which should restrict future leaks. Yet no matter what precautions are taken, the likelihood is that the *Exxon Valdez* will not be the last supertanker to fall foul of human error.

Kuwait Fires

The attack which ended the Gulf War was both stunning in its simplicity and breathtaking in its execution. With the Iraqi airforce either grounded or shot from the sky, Saddam Hussein was blind to the movements of enemy troops. His generals were totally unprepared when Allied armoured divisions performed a U-shape manoeuvre in which they moved west to attack his poorly defended southern and western flanks. Within 72 hours the world's fourth largest military force was crushed like an insect.

It was an abject humiliation for Saddam – yet even in the last hours of his doomed occupation of Kuwait he engineered a twisted revenge. As his battle-weary units retreated, leaving behind their 100,000 dead, sappers triggered Russian-made explosives planted on more than 600 Kuwaiti oil wells. The effect was cataclysmic.

Within hours smoke from the blazing well heads was thick enough to block out the sun at midday. Fireballs reared into the night sky, soot showered onto vast stretches of desert and 500,000 tonnes of oil-linked pollutants were pumped into the atmosphere every day – ten times more than the whole of American industry combined. Where wells failed to ignite, oil gushed out at up to 1000 mph to produce viscous black lakes across 300 square miles of desert. For the Coalition liberators under General Norman Schwarzkopf it was a truly awesome sight.

As one British soldier put it: 'We knew Saddam might fire the wells in order to reduce visibility for our air support. But none of us imagined the effect it would have.'

It was like a scene from a science fiction movie. Most of the fires were concentrated in the Burgan oil field, the second biggest in the world. One by one the wells affected were logged by advancing troops – Wafra, Raudhaitan, Bahra, Mutriba, Minagish, Umm, Khasman, Gudair, Sabriya, Ahmadi – the list seemed endless. Together they represented an environmental catastrophe unprecedented in world history.

Throughout the spring of 1991, in the immediate aftermath of the war, the fires raged unchecked. A pall of smoke blacked out the skies above Kuwait City, bringing pain and misery to asthma and bronchitis sufferers. Every breath meant an intake of toxic chemicals such as hydrogen sulphide, sulphur dioxide, carbon monoxide and hydrocarbons.

There was nothing the front line soldiers could do about it. They had trained for war, not as firemen. Like the rest of the world, they could

Kuwait, 1991. A huge jet of fire emerges from an oil well ignited by Saddam Hussein's retreating army at the end of the Gulf War.

only stand and watch helplessly as Saddam's vandalism left its filthy mark on the landscape.

At least 30,000 birds, many of them migrating between Africa and northern Europe, were killed. In the Persian Gulf itself, marine wildlife was decimated by the 460,000,000 gallons of unrefined crude released into the sea.

It was along this eastern coast of Kuwait that Saddam had expected a major push from crack US Marine units. He intended to fire the oil with his shore based artillery at the right moment, frying the American invaders on a giant slick. It would have been a good defensive tactic. Unfortunately for the hapless Saddam it was a wasted exercise. The US fleet stayed off-shore, pounding the dug-in Iraqi forces with shells.

With Kuwait liberated, the most urgent task facing the Allies was to tackle the oilfield infernos. They called in Red Adair, the legendary Texan fire-fighter who specialises in gusher blazes. It was Adair who extinguished the flames on the British Piper Alpha oil rig in the North Sea, a disaster which cost more than 100 lives. He was vastly experienced. But nothing he'd seen could have prepared him for his task in Kuwait.

Adair's team had no magic fix for putting out the fires. Their approach was slow and methodical, but by no means always immediately successful. Millions of gallons of water would be pumped on to the flames while giant robotic cranes, protected by heat-deflecting shields, would slowly inch towards them. Then a specially-shaped steel mould would be lowered on to the gaping well to snuff the fire out. Alternatively, Adair had the option of dynamite to blow them out.

The next step would be to cap the well. Adair's team used a bizarre valve nicknamed the 'Christmas Tree' which could be inserted into the gusher and then gradually closed up. It was delicate, hazardous work in appalling conditions. Every fireman on the job more than earned his £600 per day wages.

In an interview during the massive operation Adair responded angrily to criticism that sealing the wells was taking too long. He said:

'Each one in its own right would be a disaster. And we have hundreds of them to deal with. We have to improvise every step of the way – there is nothing cast in stone about how each one must be tackled. People who say we are not working fast enough don't know the power that we are dealing with. The job is as tough as hell and we are working seven days a week.'

Eventually, Adair and his men won their battle. But attempts by scientists to understand the environmental consequences are still in their infancy. Some pessimists believe the smoke could cause a so-called 'nuclear winter' in some parts of the world as it rises into the upper atmosphere and blocks off sunlight.

The long-term effect on human health is also uncertain. The smoke carried many known cancer-causing chemicals and there are fears that new born babies could be born with genetic defects for many years ahead. The simple truth is that no one knows for sure.

The problem facing the scientists was summed up by climatologist Dr Hassan Nasrallah.

'We are talking about massive pollution of a kind that has never been monitored before,' he said. 'The world has no experience of a conflagration of the kind which has engulfed Kuwait. Humankind has done this awful thing to the planet and humankind will have to see what permanent damage has been done.'

For the Kuwaitis, the chaos left by the invading force can be repaired. The economic damage caused by the loss of £125 billion worth of oil may have more far-reaching consequences. From Saddam's point of view, Iraq's last act of defiance was a masterstroke. The scenes of destruction inflicted on the hated Kuwaiti rulers were shown regularly on TV. With a little propaganda spin from Baghdad, thousands of Iraqis really began to believe that they had won the war.

One of many firefighters struggles to plug a burning well in the Burgan Oil Field.

Oil spill victim – the toxic crude binds the bird's feathers and feet. Thousands of animals died after Saddam's attack on the region's delicate ecosystem.

The Estonia

The sinking of the *Estonia* with the loss of more than 900 passengers and crew was Europe's worst peacetime disaster since the Second World War. After the horrors of Zeebrugge, nobody really believed such a tragedy could happen again. The fact that it did, once more called into question the basic design of roll-on-roll-off vehicle ferries. For those with no knowledge of marine engineering it seemed incredible that such a bulky vessel could sink inside 45 minutes. The problem was that once water breached the cargo decks of the vessel there were no bulkheads which could be sealed off. Waves were free to run the length of the ship's interior, destroying her balance. Yet perhaps the most shocking aspect of the *Estonia* disaster was that for dozens of passengers death may have come agonisingly slowly. Experts suspect that some victims may have survived for hours, trapped in air pockets in the ship, resting on the sea bed, hoping against hope that help would come and, finally, succumbing to the unremitting, numbing cold.

In the history of disasters at sea the last voyage of the *Estonia* is among the grimmest chapters. And yet until the moment of her doom, everything about the voyage across the Baltic Sea from Tallinn to Stockholm had been boringly normal. In the *Baltic Bar* early that Wednesday morning, 28 September 1994, the Henry Goy dance band was banging out Elvis Presley and Beatles numbers for passengers who hadn't retired to their cabins. They carried on until 1 am when the rolling of the ship in gale-force winds became too much. Most of the 1,049 passengers and crew – mainly businessmen, day trippers and shoppers – were already tucked up in bed.

A few die-hard drinkers moved on to the *Pub Admiral* for a nightcap. There was still a chance to try out the karaoke machine. One group taking the microphone had been attending an on-board conference run by oil executive Thomas Grunde, 43. The delegates regarded the event as a perk and were making the most of every minute. Grunde, who was to be one of only 141 survivors, recalled what happened next: 'When we came to the end of our number there was a big bang at the front and the ship started to lean a little,' he said. 'Some were afraid, others laughed. Myself, I did not react. Then came another bang, still worse than the first, and the ship started really to lean over. I shot over the dance floor and hit my forehead on a chair or table. A friend helped me to get up, asking how I was feeling. From that moment I had only one thought: I had to get out.'

Another reveller, Altti Hakanpaa from Finland, believed his decision to take a late-night drink saved his life. 'If I had been asleep in my cabin I would, without doubt, be dead now,' he said. 'I was just about to have a drink when I felt the boat list dangerously. I realised something was wrong. I rushed to take the elevator to the top deck and the liferafts.

'I was panic stricken. I watched as the *Estonia* sank beneath the waves. It was terrible. It all happened so quickly. Around ten minutes passed between the time the ship first began to list and when it disappeared.'

It seems the *Estonia* began shipping water soon after 1 am. But perplexingly it was not until 1.26 am that the bridge sent out its first and only distress signal: 'Mayday, Mayday. We have a list of 20 – 30 degrees. Blackout. Mayday.'

Why this SOS was not transmitted earlier, and why no attempt was made to muster passengers before the situation became critical, remained two of the key questions for investigators.

As the ship went down, the pathetic cries of the dying filled the air. One survivor, Mr Heidi Auvinen, 31, recalled: 'I was thrown into the sea and tried to find a place in a lifeboat. I grabbed a rope attached to one of the lifeboats. With great effort and despite waves several metres high I was able to drag myself aboard.'

'The raging sea looked terrible, with corpses floating in the water, lifeboats, abandoned clothing. I heard distant cries for help, groaning. The memory will haunt me for ever.'

Andrus Maidre, a nineteen-year-old Estonian on a pleasure cruise with friends, witnessed the most pathetic and heartbreaking sight of all. 'Some old people had already given up hope and were just sitting there crying,' he said. 'I also stepped over children who were wailing and holding on to the railing.'

Among the first ships to answer the Mayday was the ferry *Isabella*. One of its passengers, Swede Mr Hemming Eriksson, painted a dreadful picture of the carnage that confronted him. 'There were hundreds of bodies that were bobbing up and down in the sea,' he said. 'Many were dressed only in underwear and life vests. Some of them moved, so you could see they were living, but we had no chance to bring them up in the heavy sea. The worst was when the bodies got sucked into the propellers.'

So what was the reason for the *Estonia*'s catastrophic sinking? All the evidence pointed to a fault in the bow doors, designed to open and close for the loading of vehicles. Bow doors were blamed in the *Herald of Free Enterprise* disaster at Zeebrugge. But whereas the error which doomed the *Herald* was down to a sleeping crewman and lax on-board safety systems, it was not immediately obvious why the *Estonia*'s doors had failed.

One theory was that they had been smashed open by the intense battering-ram action of the sea. Rune Petterson, an expert in marine hydraulics, had carried out work on the *Estonia* in 1988 when she was named the *Sally Viking*. He pointed out that both the bow visor and the vehicle ramp – which forms an inner door when it is raised – were locked in place by the same hydraulic system.

'A leak in a cylinder or valve could have made the holding pressure sink, thereby making one or more locks lose their grip on the visor,' he said. 'The gaskets in the big lifting cylinders have to take the full pressure and then they may have been torn away from their fastenings. The result would be a loosening of the locks on the inner door as well, allowing the sea to drive into a narrow opening. If this was indeed the case, the force of water entering the ship would be almost incomprehensible. A gap of one square meter, and water entering at a speed of ten metres a second, would mean that in one second ten tonnes of water would have got in. In the space of a minute, the ship would have taken on 600 tonnes.'

The Estonian government was reluctant to accept this theory, believing it compromised both the integrity of the ship and her crew. Johannes Johannson, managing director of the ferry's owners, Estline, pointed out that 40 old wartime sea mines had been found near the island of Osmussaar, which lay many miles to the south-west of the *Estonia*'s last known position.

His hypothesis of an explosion was backed by the ferry's third engineer, Margus Treu. Mr Treu said: 'I was in the engine room and then I heard two or three strong blows, as though the ship had sailed into a wave. But these blows shook the whole ship so it was not a natural sound. This was an alien sound.'

As realisation of the disaster began to dawn in Estonia and Sweden, dozens of towns and villages were thrown into mourning.

Lindesberg, 40 miles north of Stockholm, lost 22 women – all mothers with children aged under 18. The suburb of Uppsala lost 26 of its court officials, who had been on a fact-finding mission to Estonia and at Jonkoping, south of Stockholm, 400 people packed the local church to mourn for 13 pupils and their 2 teachers who had been on a bible school outing.

The pain of the mourners was tangible. For the survivors it must have been unbearable. Not only had they watched hundreds of young lives perish but also had been totally helpless to act. Many of them felt guilty for being alive.

Unsuprisingly, symptoms of post traumatic stress disorder soon appeared.

One of those rescued was 29-year-old Kent Harstedt, a student from the University of Lund. He had rushed from his cabin when the first blow struck the ship and had found himself on deck alongside another student, twenty-year-old Sara Hedrenius. Harstedt introduced himself using his full name, an odd formality in laid-back Swedish culture. They both believe that chance meeting on the edge of disaster kept them alive. Together they clawed their way to what had become the top side of the ship. Then, before jumping into the sea, they agreed to meet in a Stockholm restaurant for dinner the following week.

Both of them kept the date. As Harstedt put it: 'Somewhere in this chaos we have to encourage each other.'